Global Recovery Manual

The Greatest Single Factor for Recovery is the Individual

William Houston

ADVFN BOOKS

Acknowledgements

A book like this needs the help of a great number of people. I hope I have mentioned all the references in the text and am sorry if any have been left out. The views expressed in this book are mine alone and I apologise for any errors therein. In particular I would like to thank the help and encouragement from Larry Acker, Jonathan Arter, Evelyn Browning Garriss, Ian Gordon, Lacy Hunt, John Lawton, Stephen Lewis, Marc Nuttle, Martin Pring, Jim Puplava, Jacob Rees-Mogg, Christeen Skinner, Peter Warburton and Stephan Wrobel. I would like to give particular thanks to good friends and colleagues Richard Addis, Dick Fox, Robin Griffiths, Stephen Hill, and my printer Alan Robertson, who have all been a great source of wisdom and encouragement.

Finally I would like to thank my wonderful wife Averil who, once again, has had to endure a husband whose mind preferred to mull over ideas for saving the world instead of fulfilling his domestic duties...

St James's January 2015

Acknowledgements

CONTENTS

Introduction

The first performance of Richard Wagner's mighty operatic Ring Cycle was first held at Beyreuth during the summer of 1876. The primary story is about a gold ring with magical powers stolen from the Rhinemaidens by evil men who wished to be powerful; the opera ends with the ring being returned to its owners after the death of the hero Siegfried. There is, however, a subsidiary tale of the gods who build themselves a mighty castle Valhalla and interfere in the lives of humans. The return of the ring coincides with the destruction of Valhalla.

Now we have a more modern epic that probably started early in the last century when politicians, instead of building on existing social programmes, decided to start completely new state support plans and scrapped those that had grown up organically; the additional cost then was easily borne by taxpayers in an expanding economy. Unfortunately, well-meaning politicians continued to build on the concept that the state knew better than tradition and many more undertakings were embarked upon in health, education and welfare. This was in the belief that these programmes would always be affordable together with the cost of the people to manage them, either through taxation or by additional borrowings. It seems that nobody understood that by giving people money earned by others, rather than encouraging them to earn a living, they would create a permanent underclass that would grow when times were difficult.

There had always been economic downturns ever since Biblical times and, wise people that they were, they built them into a fifty-year cycle called the Jubilee at the end of which all debts were forgiven and onerous contracts voided. This same cycle was resurrected in 1928 when a little known Russian economist analysed data from the United States, Britain and France to arrive at a rhythm of between fifty and seventy years consisting of an upswing, a levelling out and a downwave; it was called the Kondratieff wave after its discoverer. Subsequently it was found to be caused by the increase, then the collapse of debt, during the downturn.

The last time it was tackled was during the Great Depression in the 1930s when politicians in various countries decided on a different approach to the unemployment during the downturn. In America FD Roosevelt embarked on public works programmes, in Britain the chancellor balanced the budget and let entrepreneurs thrive and in Germany Hitler went for re-armament; in France they dawdled between expansion and contraction. There were numerous analyses undertaken and programmes suggested should such an event ever occur again.

And now it is happening again, with total debts at least double those relative to the GDP than the 1930s, but it seems that the sound remedial programmes have been forgotten and the failures copied. Like Wagner's gods, politicians have built great physical and bureaucratic monuments to their own importance and latterly, also like the gods, they have interfered in peoples' affairs to create mass unemployment and despair in the hope of keeping alive The European Union that cannot survive a downturn of this magnitude. All downwaves create their own technologies that drive the next upswing but this is the first for five hundred years, although politicians do not realise it, that is part of a major discontinuity that is likely to end the big institutions of the industrial era.

We should all be aware of the events around 1500 for this was the earlier watershed that, amongst other things, changed the very notion of individual freedom for millions. Fifty years either side of this date there was the invention of the movable type printing press, the fall of Constantinople to the Ottoman Turks, civil wars in England and Spain, new technologies, mega-inflation from imported gold in Spain, a major climatic shift and the Reformation that broke the power of the then Catholic church in much of northern Europe. Two hundred years later some of these events were to drive the industrial revolution and the start of the era of big power, money and government – the end of which we are now witnessing because it can no longer be afforded and is also outdated. Wagner would have understood!

So now we are faced with a similar set of conditions to the discontinuity half a millennium ago. There is militant Islam, new (particularly communication) technology, the threat of climatic shifts, likely wars over resources and immense debts that will never be repaid and will have to be extinguished somehow; there is also the printing of money that brings to mind the collapse of Weimar Germany. Although many would wish it, we will not return to the era of bigness, management and control beloved by politicians. The immense changes will bring the size of government down to what it was very early in the last century – and immense power and opportunity will be granted to the individual in the internet age – just like returning the ring to the Rhinemaidens.

How the transition is to be managed is the purpose of this manual which is based on at least nine principles:

- History shows it is futile to apply deflationary pressures to a nation without allowing the currency to float, as exemplified in the EU's Eurozone.
- Debts can only be extinguished by a. Repayment, b. Accommodation, c. Default and d. Inflation. It appears that although d. could be chosen, the most likely course will be currency devaluation and debt repayment. Any solution will destroy credit and lead to a deep recession.
- We are living in a climatic syndrome which drives 'soft' commodities upwards; applied to a depressed economy, this will cause stagflation.
- Individuals, either singly or in groups, take a nation out of recession, not the government. The best politicians can do is to provide a stable economic climate.

- Similar periods of history suggest that the present conditions will continue to engender nationalism and often conflicts; this is why anyone taking major decisions should understand its relationship to the past and the folly of reducing the armed forces.
- The best parallels to the present are the events fifty years either side of the year 1500. As is happening today, this caused a major discontinuity in the majority of lives.
- It is always wise to take remedial action before this is forced upon one and applied in panic.
- When cutting costs it is essential to define the interface between any organisation and those it aims to serve, then determine the overheads necessary to manage the new structure.
- Always arrange a recovery from the bottom up. The Digital Age will demand a new paradigm.

The guide is organised in six parts:

Part 1. Defines the major headwinds being experienced and the pressures arising from the rise of the individual.

Part 2. Discontinuity and the Learning Curve defines how much faster reactions are needed in times of distress and how these may be applied politically and in business.

Part 3. Managing the Discontinuity of the State is a four chapter programme for reducing the cost of the state, managing unemployment, helping the individual adapt to the Digital Age and creating an environment for entrepreneurs.

Part 4. The Political and Business management of hyperinflation/ hyperstagflation and depression.

Part 5. The Technologies Driving the Digital Age.

Part 6. One man's Understanding of the Digital Age.

Afterword.

Part 1.
The Headwinds

The world is beset by at least three virulent rhythms:

- Excessive debt that needs to be extinguished before a durable recovery is possible.
- Climatic conditions that are similar to those that have triggered major discontinuities in the past.
- Conflicts over water and major civil unrest.

There is one benign force: the release of individual energy sponsored by the Digital Age.

We need to go back in time to understand the import – and impact – of these forces illustrated by the composite (Diagram 1).

This is primarily a combination of the first two rhythms with their implications – and what is likely to lie ahead for the same forces, present during the 17th and early 19th centuries, are with us today. Each were periods of considerable change and distress for many but, as the descriptions that follow suggest, each heralded a new era of prosperity and new thinking.

Two major cycles that need to be understood and overcome are the 178.8 year climatic cycle and the debt rhythm of the Kondratieff Wave; the trigger of conflict are decided by these, and other forces. Finally there is the enduring nature of personal change in individuals and societies.

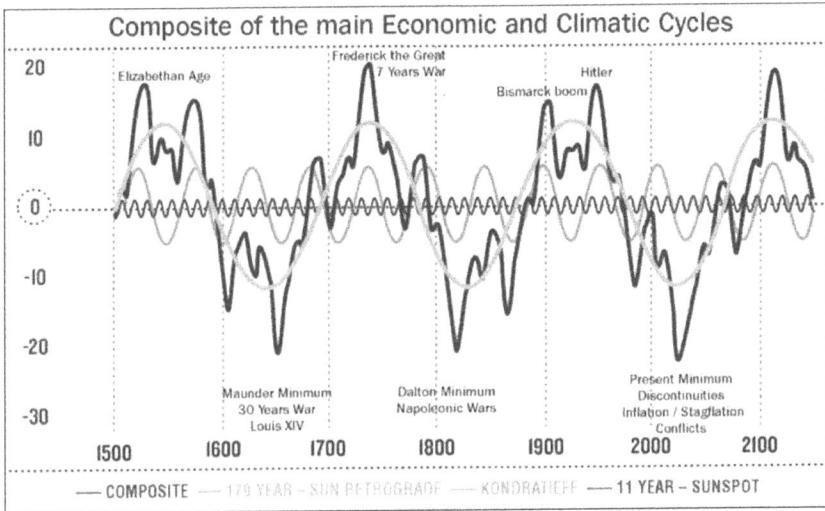

Diagram 1: the composite cycles

The 178.8-year climatic cycle shown in Diagram 2 is based on the reaction of our planet to major shifts in the solar system. It is thought that the imbalance of the great planets Jupiter and Saturn has at least two effects. The first is to distort the sunspot cycle to reduce the solar output, the second is to drive long-term tidal forces to the northern hemisphere shown in the solid orange line of the chart; these act on the sensitive areas particularly around the Pacific where, in many places, the oceanic contraction causes what is known as the 'ring of fire'.

Large volcanic eruptions have the impact of thrusting millions of tons of dust and gases into the stratosphere that cools the earth surface as shown in the thin green line on the diagram; sometimes the effect coincides as shown around 1300 and 1800, other times there is a lag as in the mid-15th and 17th centuries and now. The distortions in the solar system took place on 20 April 1990 and we are only feeling the seismic effect early in the 21st century.

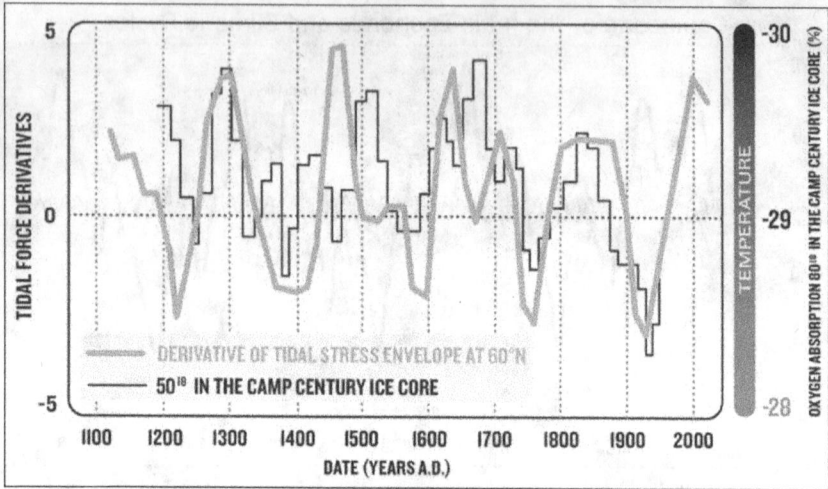

Diagram 2: the 180-year cycle – Nature 1974: Browning

We should note the interesting events that occurred at similar times to ourselves but first we should be aware of the unusually warm period in the early part of the 13th century where the weather was balmier than now but without the excess of man-made carbon dioxide that is causing so much concern today. However, it is the peaks that should interest us for these generate the headwinds that we need to understand, and counter, in the early years of the 21st century. They are called Minima, but after very difficult times there was always an upside.

- The Wolf Minimum of the 14th century devastated Western Europe to cause terrible famines in 1317/8 and later; this reduced peoples' immune system and they were unable to counter the Black Death. It was so cold it forced the evacuation of the Danish settlement on Greenland but the upside was that the frozen ground and reduced population ended serfdom in England.
- The Sporer Minimum actually occurred mid-15th century but its impact was felt around 1500 when civil wars and famines probably increased the wrath of northern Europe when the Pope excommunicated a little known Augustinian monk, Luther, who

triggered the Reformation. Then the next upside was the Elizabethan age in England.

- The Maunder Minimum started mid-17th century and lasted for 120 years. It was probably the most powerful for it was a contributory cause of the civil wars in England and in Germany, famines in the Ottoman Empire (when two Sultans were garrotted), the overthrow of the Ming Dynasty and nearly the loss of the Cape Cod colony. However, the Glorious Revolution of 1688 created the basis for the English Constitution and the Enlightenment.

- The Dalton Minimum of the late 18th century caused famines in Western Europe and was the direct cause of the violence of the French Revolution and the Napoleonic Wars. It also defeated the French Emperor in his ill-fated invasion of Russia. However, the outcome was peace in Europe until the 1870 Franco-Prussian War.

- And now? We have the prospect of wars over water, rising nationalism, mass movements of people, revolutions and civil wars. And the upside? The prospect of a new Elizabethan Age in the Digital Era.

The Debt, or the Kondratieff Cycle

The Kondratieff Cycle is the cycle of debt shown for the United States in Diagram 3. The Kondratieff long wave was called after its originator, an economist at the Academy of Agriculture in Moscow during the 1920s. Fascinated by the variations of interest rates, raw and finished goods material prices in the United States, France and Britain, he defined a cycle length of between 45 to 70 years of boom and bust caused by the rise, then destruction of debt. Of the three cycles shown in Diagram 3 only what-are-known-as K2, 3 and the not-completed 4 are shown (there was a similar period between 1790 and 1849). We should note what happened to the former periods in the US for it has great relevance for the present.

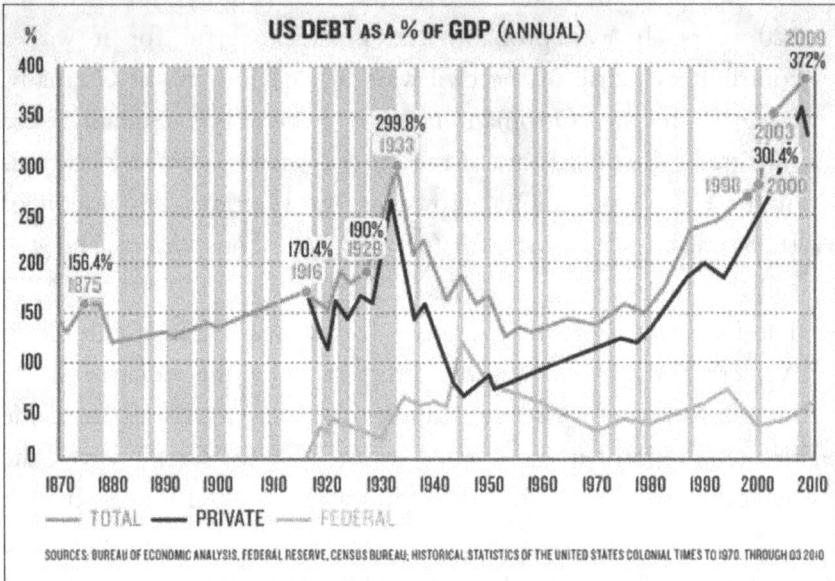

Diagram 3: the debt/GDP cycle of the USA – Courtesy: Hoisington

- The Second Cycle K2 was triggered after the Mexican War in 1842 when New Mexico, Arizona and California were ceded to the Union. The resulting gold rush added liquidity that helped the advance of banking, the building of railroads that united east and west, and the advance of agriculture. The Civil War in the early 1860s ended in inflation and a rise of debt that Diagram 3 shows collapsed in the early 1880s.

- The trigger for K3 was technology-driven with cars like the Ford Model-T, the exuberance of Theodore Roosevelt's presidency and production for the allies war machine. This ended in the rapid inflation of the 1920s followed by what was known as the 'Roaring Twenties' fuelled by excess money injected into speculation of land and stocks. This all ended in the 'crash' of 1929 followed by the nominal GDP of the US declining 50% by 1932. This explains the rise in the debt/GDP ratio to 300% in

1930 and then the crash by one third until 1935 when much of the debt nearly equal to the GDP in 1929 was destroyed. By 1950 the ratio had virtually halved.

- The start of K4 was initiated by the need to rebuild Europe and Japan, the great Marshall Plan and then the Korean War. These were the days of full employment and booming production financed by equity and debt when America was able to sell to a beleaguered world. The ratio was similar to the rise in K3 until it accelerated in the 1980s when the US outdid the USSR in weapon development to defeat communism. There was a deep recession in the early 1990s after which the Federal Reserve Bank made money freely available and the ratio exceeded the peak of 1933 in 2003.

Before a durable recovery is possible the world is faced with the prospect of needing to destroy total debt and unfunded obligations that are at least double that of 1929; many other countries are in a similar position. How to cope with such a potential catastrophe is the subject of many current essays and publications. (See www.globalrecoverycenter.org.)

The Cycles of Conflict

The cycles of conflict have been driven in the past by the two previous dynamics:

- As suggested earlier, climatic cycles have been responsible for wars over water and, what is more alarming, civil wars and revolutions.
- Depressed economic conditions have created rising nationalism and wars of expansion by states driven by dictators as a means of relieving internal unrest.

The Digital Age, the power of the individual and a 500 year cycle.

The Sporer Minimum in the early part of the 16th century was the focus of innovation, wars, exploration and, with the Reformation, particularly in England, a release of the human spirit that drove the Elizabethan Age and beyond. The technology known then drove the Industrial Revolution two centuries later; it spawned a spate of experimentation both intellectually and practically during the 18th century enlightenment that generated the huge advances of the Victorian era.

Now the technology is different. Instead of being based around the melting, rolling, forming and machining of metals it is centred around the exploitation of the atom to create a whole series of innovations that will drive the next upswing. Already communications allow the individual to access material and ideas that would have astounded their grandparents. Instead of relying on the printed word, people can now scour the internet and create movements that are enabling would-be leaders to form political parties totally outside the mainstream.

At present politicians and bankers are applying conditions on debtor counties that are forcing businesses to close, millions to be without work and rising distress, but this will change. Soon the electorate will be choosing individuals to represent them with views and policies that directly affect individual lives – just as the Reformation freed the human spirit from the then control of the Roman Church. The resources now available to the individual are forcing those in power to make changes from the bottom-up, not the present obsolete top-down brutalised forces applied in many countries; what was possible only a few years ago is no longer becoming acceptable. Once again, these changes are releasing the power of the human spirit only equalled 500 years ago.

Part 2.
Discontinuity and
the Learning Curve

Introduction

The Introduction and Part 1 made it very evident that we are entering a period of high uncertainty when the immediate past is unlikely to be a guide to the future. This will be on the scale of wartime when the rapid response to a changed situation could decide the fate of any remedial program. One has only to read an account of the Battle of the Atlantic during the Second World War to realise how closely the conflict was fought and the vital importance of intelligence and rapid response.

It is always the case that the aggressor in a conflict is better prepared, which is why in the first few months, even years, of war the defenders take some time to react to a new situation; however, the response is often more sophisticated than that of the belligerent because it is forged in the heat of battle. In a sense this is also true of business where, in a marketing or acquisition situation, the response to a rapid change can be quite devastating, depending on the ability of the competitor, or target, to respond.

What helps immeasurably is if the recipients have a sense of history which is why business schools teach case studies and why anybody in authority should understand the environment in which any upset takes place and how similar events have turned out.

This is why this guide is at pains to locate the present in an historical context and cite as many case histories as possible so that the reader, confronted by a new situation, will be better able to respond. The purpose of this chapter is to identify the nature of feedback and to suggest ways in which any organisation, public or private, might be trained to react to alternate situations.

Part 2 Chapter 1.
Discontinuity and the Learning Curve

"The dogmas of the quiet past are inadequate to the stormy present... As our case is new, so we must think anew, and act anew. We must disenthrall ourselves and then we shall save our country."

Abraham Lincoln, 1862

Summary

This part describes how managers with any sort of responsibility should change their approach in the face of major discontinuities in the months and years to come. It suggests why this should take place, the problems to be overcome and ideas for dealing with the transition.

Introduction

In the third week of September 2008, when major institutions were either being made bankrupt – Lehman Bros. had just collapsed – forcibly acquired or nationalised, a management award ceremony was being held in London. The chairman, himself a senior president, praised the recipients for their diligence in passing the Institute of Directors exams, their knowledge of corporate governance and stakeholder responsibilities, but failed to even mention the fate of Lehman!

Clearly not a student of Bismarck, who famously said, "while other people learn from their own errors, I learn from other people's mistakes," he totally failed to warn those present that they were at the beginning of a major learning curve when managing turbulence would be the norm. One of those attending was reminded of the terrible early months of World War One when a French general ordered his officers in white pantelons, blue tunics and drawn swords, to make cavalry charges against German machine guns.

Had our erstwhile chairman been a student of the learning curve he might have rewritten his speech as follows:

"Ladies and gentlemen, I congratulate the award winners on their diligence and hard work in passing their exams but the events of this week have shown that when you return to your businesses you will be just at the foothills of a unique learning experience that will test to the limit the techniques you have learned, your ability to adapt and, quoting Joseph Schumpeter, 'Anyone can make money when demand exceeds supply. It takes brains to be successful when the reverse happens. Let me explain why...' "

The diagram in the previous chapter (Diagram 3) shows the stated total debt/GDP ratio of the US from 1870 to 2010 – to include what may be described as the tail-end of third and much of the fourth Kondratieff Long Waves (the cycles described in Part 1). Please observe the peak in the curve when the US economy declined by 50% after 1929, then the debt crashed as some $100 billion (just less than the GDP in 1929) was wiped off. Now the stated ratio is at least double that of 1929, and nearly an adjusted eight times if all federal obligations are included. A similar position exists in many countries with unfunded liabilities. An equivalent crash could wipe out debt twice the current GDP (that is near $14 trillion) or over $30 trillion – a sum that would destroy anyone unwise enough to own debt. Our American friends are not alone; we can expect a similar decline in UK debt.

You may not be aware of climatic cycles that could be every bit as important as the economic rhythms you may have been taught. These are primarily ocean oscillations that became very difficult around the turn of the century, a capricious sunspot cycle and increased volcanic activity. These may affect important areas of the world with drought and restricted food supplies to cause refugee movements and lead to wars. Let me summarise just some of the changes to be encountered.

Central banks' attempts to stave off deflation by flooding markets with liquidity could be aborted by a major national or corporate collapse, or a bond buyers' strike. The mammoth rise in money plus potential rise in food and energy costs could ignite raging stagflation with the possible results:

- The GDP in the early 1930s declined by 50%; this could be exceeded as the current debt levels work themselves out.
- The climatic shifts will not only support high food prices but increase the risk of conflicts and mass movements of people.
- The economic and climatic shifts will create unendurable pressures on structures such as the European Union – and will those who break away revert to conditions similar to the 1930s?
- How will Russia and China adapt to the new environments to force new alignments in the West?

Discontinuity

Chambers Dictionary describes discontinuity as a 'lack of continuity or cohesion' which might be applied to a major stock market trend reversal, a rapid rate of inflation, a change in climatic trends or the transition from peace to war. One could extend the definition by introducing some idea of time, for this chapter is concerned with the nature of the response to the long term changes described in the Introduction. We will be considering how the nature of thinking adapts to a change in direction and how it might be possible to accelerate the process. So how may some of these factors be defined?

- The threat from militant Islam could come from at least four sources: a major terrorist outrage on the US, France or UK, renewed fighting between Israel and her neighbours, an attack by Iran on her neighbours to gain renewable water sources (see below) and an attack on Iran to neutralise nuclear weapons. In addition to revolutions in North Africa, we can visualise wars over water in the Punjab, Kashmir and in the Far East, over both rice and water.

- It is a commonplace that traditional manufacturing could mostly disappear from the industrialised West to the East through globalisation; this is being challenged by technology but the new ideas will employ many fewer people. Unfortunately these changes could create a pool of permanent unemployment, particularly in young men, which would be a disaster for them and would cause major social problems.

- The last major pandemic occurred at the end of the First World War with the Spanish 'flu that killed more people than the conflict. The history of major epidemics suggests that the crowded conditions in many cities and rising refugee levels could generate a new wave of serious epidemics.

- What could happen should the cost of oil exceed $200/barrel?

- A failure of a major bank triggering a systemic default.

Of course, all these may not occur at the same rate, or time – or indeed be inevitable – and one can only guess which one could happen first or would be the most serious. Historically, pandemics have devastated societies or nations more quickly than other dynamics but then the capability to take countermeasures has also increased. What is the mindset that either rejects the possibility of these events happening or – taking Bismarck's boast – "While other people learn from their own errors, I learn from other people's mistakes" – how can we learn from others?

In his excellent *Introduction to Nanotechnology* Eric Drexler describes how the replicating process in cells applies also to human mental patterns as 'memes' (rhymes with creams) – a term originated by Richard Dawkins, an Oxford zoologist. These are processes whereby ideas, tunes, fashions, writing and thought patterns are passed, most of the time, by the process of imitation. They pass from parent to child and, if they work, form part of a credo. For example, the stock market bullish phase lasted, albeit with some retrenchments, from 1932 to 2001 – a passage of nearly three generations! Anyone believing this trend would have made money most of the time. Unfortunately lies, bad theories or rumours also have a habit of being replicated. One example, described in the former chapter, is that Keynsian spending will trade an economy out of recession.

Memes generate their own immune systems, like a body rejects pathogens. Drexler suggests that the oldest and simplest immune system 'believes the old and rejects the new'. It was why the Catholic Church rejected the Galileo sun-orientation theories and would have burnt him as a heretic had he not recanted. This thinking is not confined to the Church; every large organisation has a built-in rejection mechanism to anything that conflicts with its core credo.

Even so, Drexler suggests that reject-the-new has real advantages for there are traditions that have been tried and found to work. The American Constitution drawn up in 1793 may have been extended by Supreme Court judgements but the principle of checks and balances in the system has never been successfully challenged. With all this inertia to change, how is it possible that people can respond to change (or threats), for the good new ideas to be accepted and for a genuinely new direction to be embarked upon?

One can only marvel how Pharaoh accepted Joseph's dream interpretation of the seven good years of abundance then seven bad years of famine as a remarkable instance of understanding, leading to action. That the Nile had seriously ebbed was part of Egyptian history that made Joseph's forecast of a famine more credible.

A remarkable anticipation of war and action in the face of a potential threat must be the creation by the Royal Air Force of the Chain Home Low (CHL) system around Britain by 1939. This was a method of radar reporting, fighter alerting and vectoring that made victory at the Battle of Britain possible. Low frequency radar had been developed and tested in the mid-to-late 1930s but it was the genius of Hugh Dowding to integrate it into a complete system of detection and fighter direction. Despite the weapon-proving ground of the Spanish Civil War, the other services were relatively unprepared for the new warfare. The previous war influenced the Royal Navy to believe that the main action would be against ships, not from the air and, despite pioneering the tank, the British army had nothing to counter the German panzers.

Like genes, ideas also split and combine to take different and multiple forms then themselves replicate but, as we saw with Pharaoh, they need a receptive and powerful listener to become acceptable. One remarkable instance of a lone voice was that of Winston Churchill who, during the 1930s, created his own 'think tank' from his home at Chartwell, so concerned was he about the Nazi war build-up. However, he failed to make any headway against an obdurate government until Neville Chamberlain was convinced of the threat. A knowledge of history must make us familiar with possibilities – as presumably Pharaoh was with droughts. It helps people accept at least the probability of a discontinuity.

All the potential changes in direction considered earlier had historical portents so why are not more people taking greater notice of the dynamics set out in Part 1? All have happened in some form before – such as the Weimar German Inflation or the Great Depression. But perhaps Drexler's concepts of an ideas-immune system makes it easy for us to reject external threats as probably being too difficult to deal with in the hope they may never happen, or just go away! The recent TV debates during British elections were a case of denial, with each participant determined to dodge reality.

A further insight into the possibility of why change is resisted in the face of a threat is what behavioural psychologists call a self-attribution bias – implying that there is a tendency for good outcomes to be attributed to skill and bad outcomes to be attributed to sheer bad luck. In an interesting paper published by the American advisor John Mauldin, James Montier observes that 70% of the time sports journalists commenting on their team's win put the outcome down to skill while 55% of the time a loss was put down to bad luck. In commenting on the Spanish Civil War, Anthony Beevor reports that the Republicans blamed disasters on imagined enemies within rather than their own shortcomings. Now the West is faced with an Arabic threat where the Koran has no word for individual responsibility, which makes it hard for believers to learn from their mistakes. One wonders what Bismarck would have made of the present combination of threats?

So what is the transition of discontinuities?

The Theory of Disbelief is well known in investing circles where there are four stages of recognising a discontinuity:

- Denial that anything is wrong, it's just a blip, 'This time it's different', nothing to worry about, do nothing about my investments.
- Anger, we will fight it, buy on the dips in the market.
- Acceptance, we have got it wrong – I'm out!
- What do I do next?

It will be apparent that this does not just apply to investors. It took Chamberlain three or four years to agree with Churchill about Hitler's menace while he went through the same process of disbelief: 'dare to contradict me, we have a deal with this bit of paper' etc, we prepare for war.

It is pointless to suggest that we can learn much more from our mistakes than from our successes unless there is some rapid corrective feedback mechanism – usually stimulated by reference to some historical event – that had been very damaging previously. Three further instances out of many: two military and one civilian, provide examples of both mistakes and the value of feedback – or the lack of it.

- Although the Supermarine Spitfire could out-manoeuvre its opposite number the Messerschmitt 109 during the Battle of Britain, it suffered from two basic defects. The first was that its Merlin engine was fitted with carburettors that caused a flame-out during certain manoeuvres; the second was that it was only fitted with .303 machine guns while the ME 109 could outrange it with 20mm cannons. Both these advantages could have been avoided if the Air Staff had been aware of the German experience of air battles against Russian fighters during the Spanish Civil War. After that, considerable efforts were made to correct the defects.

- During the Norwegian Campaign a British carrier unit was waylaid and sunk by the Battle Cruisers Scharnhorst and Gneisenauer despite the Admiralty being aware of the enemy's presence, through Ultra. The disaster could have been avoided had the senior officer recalled the success of Room 40 in the Admiralty in breaking the German Navy's codes in the previous Great War. There is little doubt that after this disaster future commanders listened to the intelligence intercepts.

- Herbert Hoover was regarded as one of the best qualified American presidents when he was elected in 1928. His experience of mining in many parts of the world and his wartime food relief programme had given him a global perspective. As Secretary of Commerce he had won acclaim for his work on the Mississippi flooding. However, as president, he failed to recognise the deflation of the 'thirties that had been forecast by a little known Russian economist with a sense of history. He even brought into play the Reconstruction Finance Corporation (RFC) designed to bail out failing banks that his successor used to underwrite people, enterprises and local authorities.

In the first two cases, the feedback was rapid and decisive because war brings a great sense of urgency. In the third, Hoover could have had a Joseph to warn him that there had been at least two depressions in the previous century, and to describe their effects. However, there are cases when they can be de-stabilising. In work done by Dr Harry Nyquist, an American physicist majoring on servo-systems, it was postulated that excessive feedback would be de-stabilising and create self-destruction. If too weak, however, the mechanism would respond sloppily. Clearly wartime conditions need a much faster feedback than peacetime – although the possible events postulated earlier could change this perception.

It is for this reason that peace-time threats, from whichever direction, are seldom acted upon until they become a painful reality. The carrier admiral was likely to have been an intelligent man but seemed unaware that there was data that could have saved his life. How then can we speed up the process and learn from others' mistakes? Is there a framework, such as scenarios based on history, within which we can at least be aware of the possibility of a discontinuity and, like Pharaoh, respond? The next sections consider how this might work.

Reducing the Discontinuity and Learning Curve:

The transition from peace to war probably represents the most testing time for those at the sharp end of a conflict with rewards for those who learn quickly and risk for those who do not. There is the story told of the commander of a light bomber squadron detailed to damage the German invasion fleet being built up in the French channel ports in August 1940. The peace-time delivery technique was for the aircraft to fly straight and level at medium height before the bombs were released – a perfect target for ack-ack gunners. In the attack the first planes which went in were mauled but fortunately the next commander survived and adapted a new technique of attack for the next raid by coming in low. He was one of a very few Air Force cadets of 1919 who survived the Battle of Britain and the war.

More recently, the armed services put those who may be in harm's way through as realistic a training period as possible before potential conflict and in so doing try to avoid fighting yesterday's battles. One such is the Royal Navy's 'work-up' unit at Portland where, on commissioning, ships are put through a strenuous and realistic series of exercises to test the crews and equipment.

One ship going through the process was HMS Invincible, whose commanding officer Captain JJ Black, Royal Navy (later Admiral Sir Jeremy Black, GBE, KCB, DSO), was one of two carriers of the task force detailed to retake the Falklands Islands seized by Argentina in 1982. Black was detailed to command the air defence of the operation.

Unlike most of the captains, Black had served in the Korean and Borneo wars so had direct experience of the intensity of conflict. His journal explains that when his ship was nominated there were two days of intense preparation before sailing. Nobody had any time for apprehension as individuals were recalled from leave and there was frantic activity to load stores and armaments. The activity was not confined to Invincible. In the time before sailing, helicopter pads were built over swimming pools in the merchant ships detailed for the landing assault and all parts of the services were brought to readiness.

Jeremy Black explains how he set about bringing his ship to war status while sailing from Portsmouth down to the South Atlantic. There were periods of intense drills while dummy attacks were made on the ships to test the equipment and the response of those on board. The ships were also prepared for war with all inflammable items either stowed or ditched, as the damage control systems aimed to ensure the vessel responded to attack and fire were tried and retried.

Another innovation was to ensure that either he or his second-in-command were in the operations centre when in the combat zone by taking twelve hours on and twelve off. This meant there was a responsible officer able to take decisions at all times. A British warship that did not adopt the same procedure failed to take avoiding action from an Exocet missile and had ultimately to be abandoned and was sunk.

Black deemed that communications with the ship's company was an essential part of command. He did it personally for longer term events but under air attack he detailed an officer with an unexcitable voice to keep the crew abreast with events. This meant that as far as possible individuals below decks were not distracted from their jobs by ill-founded rumour.

The journals give some indication of the intensity of action – particularly air raids that tended to occur at the same time every day enabling everything to be in readiness, as far as possible, for the attacks, with some combat aircraft airborne and others at readiness. The problem, as with all combat, was to ensure adequate readiness without over-tiring the aircrew and all those engaged in their support and direction.

The campaign showed the overall need for good intelligence. For example, after the landing at San Carlos Bay, the air defence had to be divided between protecting the landing and the task force itself. This required an understanding of the enemy's priorities for it was naturally believed that the main attack would be on the supply ships, not their escorts. As it was, although warships were sunk, the prime purpose to re-take the Islands was not unnecessarily delayed.

So how can the learning curve be applied to civilian life?

At first sight, it seems improbable that there is any parallel between military action and commerce. How can the perception of events set out earlier provide a bridge to shorten the time span determined by the Theory of Disbelief?

What then could be the civilian equivalents to Captain Black's experience described earlier? How is the board of a company to make a judgement of an event, or a trend, that might seriously impact on its future profitability or solvency? Consider some of the parallels.

The commanders: Black was clearly an exceptionally talented and experienced leader, but this was not all. Naval training is designed to prepare for conflict – as are those with MBA qualifications designed for running a business in normal times. However, as Lincoln understood, the Civil War needed a new approach – so business people need a new perspective to deal with stagflation, for example.

Business courses are unlikely to teach how to deal with significant reversals such are those experienced in the mid-1970s, early 1980s, the late 1990s and now in the early decades of the new century. For example, in the turmoil of the mid-1970s, no one on the board of a wallpaper manufacturing company suggested that the rhythm of quarterly board meetings be changed despite a severe contraction of business conditions; it subsequently failed.

Experienced insolvency/bankruptcy practitioners comment that when business conditions change it is often necessary to replace the chairman and chief executive before the company can start to recover.

Measuring discontinuity is more difficult than in combat conditions. As we have shown earlier, a major trend change can come from different conditions and timings to generate a number of different scenarios – each of which could be tracked and monitored for their degree of seriousness. When a new trend occurs, this would be noted at the highest level and the agenda of the business changed. The banking crisis in October 2008 was just such a trend change – but memories are short lived!

Simulating discontinuity is not presently on the agenda of most company boards, but there could well be an equivalent of Portland for the Royal Navy to simulate major trend changes. For example, a board could agree that the company could be vulnerable to a certain set of scenarios; they might then submit themselves to a consultancy specialising in generating simulations and monitoring the financial and operational impact of decisions. Within a controlled environment the organisers could feed a series of possible situations into the decision-making process for the board to assimilate, discuss and respond. Those running the exercise could then evaluate the performance and suggest improvements. The same could be applied to government or other administrative agencies.

Contingency action plans may then be drawn up by the senior managers based on the alternative strategies defined by the board. Indeed, UK banks are now required to write their own Living Wills and submit them to the Bank of England.

As a result of such an exercise it may be deemed that the presently constituted board may not be the optimum vehicle for absorbing and interpreting new intelligence. They might consider creating a 'shadow board' familiar with the dynamics of the business and able to forewarn of changes from inflation/stagflation to deflation, variation in interest rates or currencies or major shifts in commodity prices – a feature dealt with in another chapter. These inputs would be fed into the model that would indicate changes in the dynamics or priorities of the business.

The training need not just be confined to businesses and to institutions. Why should not politicians subject their judgements to a similar set of possible events and for third parties to measure their impact on the nation. Indeed, the UK's ORSA now does exactly that with the Chancellor's budgets. The same would apply to individuals and one can anticipate centres being set up where personal decisions can be tested against the realities of their people's lives.

Part 3.
Managing the State
through Discontinuity

Introduction: Managing a
State in Troubled Times

The political management of the next few years will require the highest qualities of understanding, historical perspective, wisdom, brain power and character to deal with the combination of events described in Part 1 for, as suggested earlier, it will represent dealing with a discontinuity not present for decades, even centuries, and will bankrupt many states.

However, the political qualities will need to learn from business management when it comes to downsizing their organisation that was orientated more towards managing a war than peace. This is because it has undertaken functions such as health, education and welfare, imposing costs that would never be acceptable to a private organisation. This might be possible during the growth phase of a cycle when these were funded from income, but are totally unacceptable during a debt-driven downwave when only increasing debt can avoid technical insolvency. Excessive debt is the very issue preventing any lasting growth, and it will be hard for many countries to avoid a default!

Unwinding any organisation is hard and fraught with anxiety and anger at the best of times, it is even more fraught during a downwave when those made redundant would find difficulty in landing another job for a number of the skills in public service are often different from those outside. In addition, the methods presently adopted by politicians tend to apply blanket cuts to departments which often means that those people actually interfacing with the public at the bottom of the pile are the first to be fired while the original administration remains; it is as if when things 'return to normal', the organisation will resume its previous grand duties. This, as we have seen in Part 1, is unlikely to happen after a major discontinuity.

This is why this part is concentrating primarily on how individuals can be helped to enter the Digital Age while at the same time the state cost to the economy can be reduced to less than one third, not the 40 to 50% present or more in many countries. As the private, not public, sector always generates growth and jobs, and the Digital Age itself is likely to mean fewer permanent jobs, any programme needs to focus on encouraging self-employment. There are four chapters which should be undertaken before entering the most dangerous stage of the credit cycle when the collapse of credit always leads to a depression.

Chapter 1. Preparing the State for the Digital Age (DA) – It is private enterprise that drives recovery, not the state.

Chapter 2. Valuing the Individual in Society.

Chapter 3. Adapting the Individual to the Digital Age.

Chapter 4. Creating an Environment Fit for Entrepreneurs.

Part 3 Chapter 1.
Preparing the State for the Digital Age

"Never in the history of the world has there been a situation so bad that the government can't make it worse"
Anon, quoted from Marc Faber GBD Report

"That government is best when it governs least... It finally amounts to this: that government is best which governs not at all!"
Henry David Thoreau

"You can always sense incompetent politicians because they emphasise spurious issues away from the critical factors"
Anon.

In 2012 the reported UK government debt was £1,023 billion and private debt £3,200 billion making a debt to GDP ratio of 272%. However, if unfunded liabilities are taken into account the state debt rises to £2,300 by raising the total to £5.5 trillion and a debt/GDP ratio to over 355%. By 2015, the ratio will be higher.

Summary

Ever since Adam Smith proclaimed that individuals spend their money more responsibly than governments, politicians have tried to prove the opposite and every time they have failed. As the above simple calculation shows, the UK, with a budget deficit of now less than 7% and total debts of 350% of GDP, is technically bust and if it was a company, the directors would be acting unlawfully if they did not call a creditors meeting.

Fortunately for them creditors have other remedies such as refusing to buy or dumping bond or gilt offerings leading to a collapse of the currency, a government default, and a drastic cut in the standard of living. Likewise, governments have the capacity to defraud their creditors as they have done many times in the past and, more recently, in Greece and Cyprus. As this chapter is concerned with preparing for the Digital Age, another simple calculation for a developed nation today will show the actual scale of the problem.

Assuming an equilibrium total debt to GDP ratio of an optimistic 200% and the present levels of around 400%, then the collapse of credit would be twice the GDP; in the US this would be $30 trillion and in the UK £3 trillion.

However, any collapse of credit on this scale would be a likely fall in the GDP of an optimistic 20% (the US GDP declined by 50% in nominal terms from 1929 to 1933 with a debt/GDP ratio half that of today) so that the collapse of credit would be a fall in debt of 2.20 times the GDP. If through inflation, this would be enough to wipe out the capital of every lending and probably also financial establishment in the land; if through deflation this would eliminate many debtors. This could never be achieved in an orderly fashion unless foreseen; it would mean cuts of socialised expenditure to achieve a government expenditure less than one third of GDP.

As the next chapter will show, it is individuals, either separately or in groups, that will propel a national recovery, not politicians. All they need is the environment to take risks. This is why a government spend of less than a third of GDP is needed, accompanied by minimum regulation at a time when politicians' instinct is to control more. Failure to do this would mean crippling debt servicing costs.

Introduction

Several studies have suggested that the Digital Age (DA) would need some 2% of the population in agriculture, 3% in government, 10% in manufacturing and around 50% in service industries. This means that perhaps 30 to 40% of the population will have no regular jobs including the underclass the welfare state has created.

This is quite different from the heyday of late 20th century when the social democratic state was so omnipotent that politicians attempted to provide a safety net through which nobody can fall. At the same time it has become wasteful, inefficient, corrupt, arrogant and incompetent. As the Bumper Book of Government Waste shows the British government wasted over £82 billion of taxpayers money out of a total government expenditure of £519 billion. It is unlikely that this is a singular occurrence.

Yet this very omnipotence probably reached its pinnacle during the Second World War. Then whole democratic states were mobilised to create armies, navies, air forces and the weapons of war. In an age of mass production the Allies, particularly the US, out-produced by around a factor of ten the total output of the Axis powers. In this the state, as never before, controlled much of economic activity and in the name of winning the war, which deprived individuals of their natural freedoms. Most willingly acceded in the name of patriotism and there was no question of unemployment because everyone was involved.

Sixty years on, little has altered in the attitude of the state but the focus and competence has changed. In wartime able people were attracted to positions where they could affect the outcome. Now politicians, many of whom with no managerial experience, aim to stay in power to the exclusion of any contribution they can make either to their constituents or to their nation.

In the UK this has been exemplified by their attitude to the banking crisis. Instead of relating back to the US Glass-Steagall Act of 1933 which separated commercial banking from investment, banks have been socialised without this essential condition of separating the two activities. This has meant leveraging the state to previously unimaginable levels in peacetime to the detriment of future generations and the state taking on totally unknown liabilities that should rightly have been managed by the market.

Unfortunately, the political debate in France and elsewhere has shown little understanding of the underlying dynamics described in Part 1, so that policies are unlikely to change unless they are forced by events. In addition, unfortunately the first reaction to a crisis will be to enlarge state control and restrict freedoms instead of implementing the sort of contingency plans described in this chapter, in anticipation.

Only in rare countries such as Switzerland has the state focussed on the four issues for which they are deemed to be responsible, such as maintaining the value of the currency, external and internal security and maintaining internal finances in equilibrium.

Any remedial policies will not just have to reduce the size of the state, because the welfare state is not working in ways claimed by their proponents. For example, *The Economist* reported that by the turn of the century there was no employment in over one-tenth of British households with children; this figure was nearer one in seven towards the end of the decade. This means presumably that in excess of three million households are underwritten by the state. The National Audit Office commentated that one in ten live in workless households. This is not singular to the countries such as the UK, as other nations such as the US, Finland, Belgium, Australia and Canada had between 10 and 15% of homes without work. This is an appalling indictment on the state's priorities.

This will not be the only problem facing the state. During deflation, it is likely that as the economy shrinks, taxed revenues will also decline which makes it all the more important that other than bureaucratic means are found to manage spending. There could also be additional pressures on the public purse such as the potential crash of housing finance, the bursting of other credit bubbles, food and medical problems, likely wars over water, increasing threat of terrorism, mass refugees and possibly also pandemics.

All these are likely to arise during the first two decades or so of the 21st century against governments already reeling from excessive borrowing. How then is the transition to the Digital Age to be made without leaving millions, at present dependent upon the public purse, destitute?

What then is to be done?

The answer probably lies in the well-tried methods of company rescue specialists who would be likely to ask the following questions:

- What areas could be safely left to the private sector in order to save costs and avoid borrowing that crowds-out private enterprise?
- How many additional responsibilities need the state undertake?
- How can entrepreneurs be encouraged for they are the people who will initiate the recovery, not the state?
- How to unwind the behemoths of both the private and public sectors?
- How is any potential unemployment problem displaced by the recession and advent of the Digital Age to be dealt with? This might be coupled with...
- How are those at the bottom of society, presently supported by the state, to be encouraged to join the mainstream?
- How can the huge build-up of debt be somehow extinguished?

All these are covered by this and other chapters.

We have been here before

Although daunting by its size there are precedents for governments reacting to hard times. For example, over eighty years ago the American credit mountain (that in those days was nearly twice the GDP – not approaching four times at present) – collapsed. This caused the real output of the United States to decline by nearly 30% while at the same time industrial production fell by nearly a half by 1932.

Unfortunately, latter-day politicians are making the same mistake as those in the 1930s through state interference, but it would be a mistake to rely on dusting off old British files. There are also at least ten similarities and differences from the past – some of which follow from Part 1:

Factor One: Commodity prices fell by over 30% from 1921 to 1937 when global oversupply was ended by poor growing conditions in the US and elsewhere with the dust bowl. This helped keep the unemployed food bills down in conditions of economic stringency. Now the climatic forces are likely to be a threat to feeding the burgeoning world population from diminishing land under cultivation, reducing carry-over stocks or conflicts disrupting supplies. Politicians might try rationing but this would only generate black markets. This, accompanied by a flat economy would create stagflation.

Factor Two: Risk of war was far from people's concerns in the early 'thirties. Although Marshall Foch had commented that the Treaty of Versailles in 1919 was a cease-fire, not a peace treaty, this was forgotten by politicians who negotiated a reduction in naval estimates and ran down the armed forces in cost-saving measures. Even when Adolf Hitler occupied the Rhineland, few paid any attention to his testament in Mein Kampf.

By late in the first decades of the new century, war in the Middle East and the potential for armed conflict over water concerning the Indian Sub-Continent and the Far East is highly likely to require an increase, not decrease, in military expenditure. This, coupled with the need for the West to increase security against terrorism, will require additional resources.

Factor Three: Banks were subject to two great failures in the 1920s and 1930s from the huge deflationary pressures. Now the situation is much more serious because banks, particularly in the Eurozone, have been buying government bond issues when the market would have been demanding much higher coupons; there are also threats from mortgage collapses in many Club Med countries and Ireland. Already Greece has had to reorganise its debt; other countries will follow.

Factor Four: Derivative exposure is an additional potential hazard from bank failure not present over eighty years ago, although trading on margin was common. These instruments, based on actual stocks, bonds, interest rates, currencies, bundles of commodities and so on, enable holders to control many times the face value of a security for a fraction of the market value.

These can be used as hedges, or as a means of speculation that proved so disastrous in the case of Barings, Lehman Brothers and AIG. It is argued that every contract has a backup but this is of little avail when banks or nations default as they did in the early 1930s. The sums are not small. By mid-2007, an estimate of the derivative value was over $600 trillion – around ten times the global GDP.

Factor Five: Housing mortgages were a problem to many Americans in 1933 with repossessions reaching a thousand a day – a rate that was hard for those involved but was not nationally calamitous. Then the problem was solved by a state-run organisation called the Home Owners Loan Corporation (HOLC) that re-financed mortgages. By the early 2012 the total mortgage exposure in the US was over $10 trillion and in Britain was approaching £1,000 billion – both over two thirds of their respective GDPs; other countries such as Spain and France have similar exposures. Taking the early 1930s decline as a yardstick, this could mean that in a major deflation a fall of house prices of around 50% over five years could imply debt repudiations of $4-5 trillion for the US and £4-500 billion for the UK. The 50% may be optimistic; in Japan it reached 80% in some areas during the 1990s.

Factor Six: Energy prices. By early 2015 energy prices have more than halved. However if Factor Two becomes a reality this could rapidly reverse.

Gas and oil energy occupy around 15% of people's spending. Should, for example, the oil price rise greatly exceed $120 a barrel then this would reduce total spending by up to 5%; any blockage of the Straits of Hormuz could put the figure at over $200. The decline in disposable income would have a devastating impact on Western-style economies. Increasing taxes would have the same impact.

Factor Seven: Inexperience. Seventy years ago most politicians had either wartime or managerial experience that, irrespective of their policies, made them competent national leaders. The same is untrue now, when few national leaders have either worn uniform or have been successful business people. This has led to political corruption, incompetence and waste in many Western countries that has undermined confidence in most politicians. This might mean that some third party could emerge as a new leader.

Factor Eight: Unemployment. Any large migration into Europe, Britain and the US will cause very considerable unemployment with the likely economic turmoil described earlier. During the 1930s depression there was considerable unemployment on both sides of the Atlantic but the jobs were still there when it was over. Now with many jobs migrating to the East, and the new technologies requiring fewer people, there will be fewer well-paid management jobs. This will cause potential social and economic problems that will have to be addressed to avoid social unrest.

Factor Nine: Demographics. For a nation to remain 'solvent' every woman needs to have at least two children; below this, countries such as Russia, Germany and Japan have declining populations while, in the period where there was abundant rainfall, there was a population explosion in India, China, Africa and many Muslim countries. At the same time those in the West are living longer with life expectation approaching the upper seventies. Among the developed world the US has a fertility rate of 2.1 and still welcomes skilled migrants.

The need to import 750,000 skilled migrants a year is particularly important in a country such as Germany with its rapidly aging population; however, many developed countries have a generous welfare programme that formerly has attracted migrants needing economic support. With the welfare programme described later, this is likely to seem less attractive.

Factor Ten: Mass migrations and pandemics were not a problem in the 1930s although the First World War saw both – the first as the result of war, the second the terrible influenza epidemic of 1918 that felled more people than ever died in the trenches. Although there is little Western deprivation that helped the H1N1 virus to spread, this is certainly not true should it hit the poor areas of Africa and Asia. As suggested in Part 1, there are climatic conditions similar to those that caused mass migrations and pandemics in the past.

Essential moves to bring the State into the Information Age

By early 2010 several libertarian solutions were being offered. Some of the most helpful are those suggested by Charles Murray in a book called *In Our Hands* who believes considerable bureaucratic expense could be reduced. Newt Gingrich, a previous House Speaker considers the implication of the futurist Alvin Toffler's Third Wave in his *To Renew America*. Other sources are mentioned later. However, the climatic and economic forces described in Part 1 demand a more radical approach.

Some new principles of procedure to change an ailing state

Any private company rescue programme has to improve cash generation and strengthen the balance sheet to be successful. Rescuing a failed state needs to work on the same principles. There are at least ten stages based on tried practice that a company recovery consultant would employ when tackling an organisation that was in danger of running out of money either through incompetence or through external pressures. In most cases this means going back in time to assess when and where the structure went wrong and, where possible, to revive the driving force before the state took control. This is how the principles may be applied to recovering the state:

Stage One: Stop cash haemorrhaging. Stop all public service recruitment, and cease all but essential travel, terminate most outside consultancy contracts and paid advisors (such as most quasi-government groups in Britain, QUANGOs). Institute a pay freeze.

Stage Two: Define what the state is for. Before the 20th century it was to maintain the value of the currency, secure national defence, enforce the laws of the land and balance public finances. The optimum state take should be less than a third of GDP. In Britain in the 1930s it was 32.8% and in 1900 10%! In Britain today it is still in excess of 40%.

Stage Three: Unwind the obvious loss-makers. Today most governments would privatise education, welfare and health as being the greatest embarrassment and ones that could be perfectly well provided privately but at the same time, ensuring a service for the least able. Some proposals are set out later.

Stage Four: Concentrate on streamlining the remaining activities such as foreign affairs, external and internal security and the treasury departments; the latter by simplifying the tax system. Also use information technology to sub-contract routine functions to specialist agencies.

Stage Five: Give maximum impetus to deregulating private industry and encouraging entrepreneurs. Historically it is only individuals working either singly or in groups that drive an economy out of recession and into the Information Age. These are dealt with in the next chapter.

Stage Six: Unwind all support for the private sector except for the commercial banks – and even those after shedding their investment arm. Introduce the modern equivalent of the US Glass-Steagall Act to dispose of failed institutions.

Stage Seven: Assess how the most endangered and vulnerable in society could be cared for outside the state system. There has been a history of private care within the community in English-speaking countries that could be revived together with charities such as the Salvation Army. As a sound principle, existing agencies should be strengthened wherever possible.

Stage Eight: Strengthen the essential services defined under Stage Two and provide the most economical means of coping with the pressures set out earlier.

Stage Nine: Determine the state or private financing policies required. Simplify system of taxation to make it comprehensible to non-specialists. Bring public service pensions into the private sector and unwind liabilities such as off-balance sheet financing.

Stage Ten: Manage the transition. There remains excessive debt. Historically this can only be extinguished through default, currency destruction or inflation. All will probably be employed in the years ahead to undermine the credit system and fiat currencies.

Fortunately there are precedents for most things in life so it is helpful to look back in history and at what took place elsewhere to act as a guide. The remainder of the chapter is devoted to Stage Three.

Unwinding education

In his thoughtful book *What Comes Next*, John Pinkerton describes how the public school system in the US has let down the most vulnerable in society. By the late 1990s, 30% of pupils on average drop out of high school – the figure is nearer 60% in urban areas. This means that some twenty-seven million Americans over the age of seventeen are probably illiterate, and another forty-five million borderline; he reported that this cost the economy nearly $230 billion a year.

It is hardly surprising that in the accompanying chaos nearly 30% of all children are sent to private schools and over a million more are educated at home – and the numbers are growing at 15% a year. Recall the number of homes with no employment and the plight of many children described earlier; a similar situation almost certainly exists in other countries.

Pinkerton reports that in 1999, nearly $530 billion was being spent on public and private education and that out of 4.6 million people employed in the field only half were teachers. Why not, he suggests, give $6,000 (the then cost per pupil – probably in the form of vouchers) to parents and let them choose their own school?

Vouchers have been successfully implemented in several American states where, in controlled experiments, 15 to 20% were more likely to finish secondary education and achieve higher grades. In Sweden vouchers worth between the equivalent of $8,000 to $12,000, depending on age, have enabled students to attend schools outside their own neighbourhood and have given a huge boost to innovation and private education; it has also boosted the status of teachers who are paid a bonus for good work. Vouchers are issued to all parents to cover primary and secondary education and could be augmented privately.

On Pinkerton's principle, what he calls the Bureaucratic Operating System (BOS) means that anything the state runs is 25 to 30% more costly than when privately managed. A perfect illustration of the BOS was a paper by the OECD reporting that, despite an increase in the British National Health Service (NHS) funding from 2000 to 2006 of from £44 billion to £76.4 billion in 2005, the standard of healthcare in Britain remains below that of many countries and that in some hospitals wards are closing and doctors and nurses are being fired. In commercial terms it would seem impossible that a company nearly doubling its revenue with similar facilities, and with ample supply of funds, could still make a loss.

Unwinding the BOS inefficiencies can be applied to a school with, say 1,000 pupils. Pinkerton suggests that by becoming independent a school should be able to save over $1.5 million to be spent on better teachers, equipment, management and so on. Charles Murray in his book *What it Means to Be a Libertarian* confirms that at the turn of the century this figure was about right at that time.

Out of political control, this would create much diversity in the school system with additional revenue being raised for such things as adult and vocational classes, remedial work for those whom the state has failed and supporting the work of the Conservation and Security Agency and National Recovery Agency described later. There would be many opportunities for innovation once education was liberated from the state.

For the transition to independence there will be a need for most schools to recruit a bursar (full or part time depending upon the size) whose function would be to control the finances and manage the administration. Another would be for the school premises to be transferred to ownership of the governors so some low interest mortgage should fund the transfer from the present owners, and be paid off with the surplus funds likely to be generated.

Unwinding Health

Health has been nationalised in the UK since 1948 and partly in the US from 1965; a state-run insurance programme exists in America. Experience has shown that while the system can at its best provide good and committed healthcare, it suffers from the distortion of anything run by politicians. It also becomes an election issue when competing parties vie to spend more money, provide additional benefits, or to make the service more adaptable and so on. This only burdens the existing organisation with additional costs, targets and duties. By its very nature it requires a large bureaucracy to manage many people which makes it, in Britain, the largest employer; in Europe too it is heavily unionised, costly to run, inflexible and restricts choice.

Advances in medicine have reduced the cost of treatment for many procedures allowing patients to be released much earlier than previously. This also potentially improves productivity where remote sensing of post-operative conditions has given nurses more freedom to do their job. Also two-thirds of all Medicare costs treat chronic conditions which could be treated in separate centres devoted to better care of these ailments. However, any state system is resistant to change and innovation is discouraged unless sanctioned by the bureaucracy.

In his book *In Our Hands*, Charles Murray suggests that everyone from the age of 21 should receive a lump sum for the remainder of their lives that, for higher incomes, would be taxed. From this they would be obliged to take out medical insurance and provide for their own pensions and unemployment insurance.

The idea is for the insurance industry to offer a flat rate insurance to cover major surgery and catastrophes costing (in the early part of the decade) of around $3,000 a year, which might include a regular medical check; individuals would then pay for simple treatments from their own pocket. Murray suggests there should be no premium payable for smokers, obesity or other habits damaging to a more healthy lifestyle. This would probably be unacceptable in a more puritanical regime.

In their book *The Plan*, Carswell and Hannan suggests a modification to Murray's proposal adopted by Singapore based on a two tier system where a proportion of the sum allocated is set aside for routine treatment:

> This would require an obligatory 'savings account' where each individual is required to set aside a sum allocated for healthcare every year to pay for routine health visits; this would usually be associated with a specified general practitioner. Initially the

demand for treatment is likely to be small so the fund increases; those older people entering the programme would be given an initial 'pool'. It is held that it is in the patient's best interest to adopt a healthy lifestyle to keep the fund viable. The second is an obligatory insurance plan to pay for in-patient operations.

Carswell and Hannan argue that this plan reduces the inevitable bureaucracy associated with a state funded or wholly insurance-based system. It would also create many levels of health-care support that do not exist at present and provide the individual with considerable choice such as first-aid clinics run by paramedics. This would take over much of the accident and emergency treatment at present undertaken by hospitals. There would, however, be caveats. Providers would only accept risk for the treatment given, not some parallel tort for something unconnected with the work done.

The concept of diversity is not theoretical. *The Economist* of April 2009 describes how a multi-layered system has grown organically in India where nearly four-fifths of all care is provided either by individual firms or charities with the state contributing less than 20%. Enterprises provide the sort of diversity suggested to meet low overhead provision for different levels of treatment and expense.

Assuming the spending in the UK was over £2,000 per person in 2006/7 then taking Pinkerton's BOS penalty of 30%, the expenditure per patient is actually £1,600. Should the system be privatised then it would be possible to spend another £200 or so per patient and for the tax payer to save the same amount. As with schools, there will be a need to transfer the free or leasehold of the hospital or clinic to new owners, be they a holding company, trust or governors. As with schools, part of the funds released by a more efficient operation could be diverted to pay off mortgages, invest in new equipment or in better services.

This will be an opportunity to eliminate the role of government in education and healthcare although there may be residual units to look after such matters as organising response to catastrophes such as pandemics.

The paradox of social security

It is relatively easy to run a welfare state when economies are expanding, for there is a tacit acceptance that taxation revenues will pay for an underclass that politicians have neither the wit nor the will to disturb. This part of the chapter aims to describe the unwieldy monster that many countries have allowed to grow that cannot now be afforded and will have to be unwound in a deep recession; a later chapter sets out the practical policies that are needed while still caring for the most vulnerable in society. This section shows how allowing different life-styles presents a burden on themselves and the taxpayer. For example in Britain:

- A lone mother with a child would in 2006/7 receive total benefits, including use of a council house, of £8,939 a year. Living with her boyfriend in an undeclared relationship he would be able to claim a further £2,987 a year and be entitled to a council house that he could re-let. Should they declare their relationship or marry, there would be a loss of £1,288 a year. These figures are taken from a recent pamphlet by the Institute of Economic Affairs in London.

- This is based on the quasi-Marxist belief that each individual has a 'right' to pursue their own means of expression through their own chosen life-styles. The evidence shows that politicians have created an expensive underclass, despite all the evidence that this is to the national disadvantage.

- The proportion of single occupancy homes has doubled in the last forty-five years with half of the occupants being below pensionable age. This is now 30% of all households and could rise to 40% by 2021 and has led to an unreasonable demand for additional housing at considerable extra expense and diminution of farmland.

- Council houses in England were designed to provide the first roof over newly-wed couples and for older people; now nearly three-quarters of all these homes are occupied by single individuals, with or without children. The London Magazine calculated that the cost in supporting these arrangements is over a quarter of a million pounds per house/year.

- Women often have a baby to leave their childhood home and set up on their own causing the proportion of births out of wedlock to rise to nearly 40% in 2004. This means that a quarter of all children have lone parents. Even if the parents cohabit, their relationships are more likely to break up than married couples.

- A study showed that the children from married couples by every measure do much better than those from single-parent families and that two thirds of children by co-habiting parents will see their parents split-up by the time they are ten. This means huge transfer payments, higher levels of child poverty and worklessness in single, rather than married, households.

- On average, children from single parents, compared to a married couple, do less well at school, are more likely to be involved in criminal activities, are less successful economically and are more likely to become single parents themselves. This problem is compounded in the US because lone children are often brought up by their grandparents – 2.3 million in the 2000 census. Unfortunately many of these have low incomes, did not do well at school and often were not the best of parents themselves.

- It is a fallacy to argue that benefits follow life-style. The reverse is true. Why, for example, restrict childbirth when the state will take the place of an irresponsible parent and pay you not to work? Many men will be happy to become fathers if they have no responsibility for the outcome; one 21-year old sired children from seven women at the estimated cost to the taxpayer of a million pounds a year!

- In the US there was a mass exodus from welfare when the support was made temporary and a 36% decrease in the likelihood of unwed single mothers when housing support fell by $150; where couples were given the same rights as those living singly with children, the number of marriages increased markedly.

- For their own ends, politicians have encouraged reliance on the state accompanied by feckless and fraudulent behaviour to create client voters. In this way the taxpayer is called upon to underwrite a virtual underclass – and the loss to the economy of these seemingly willingly dependent people to the tune of approaching £20 billion p.a. with fraud costing up to £200 million p.a.

The aforementioned article in *The Economist* explains how government benign neglect turns out what sociologists call *status zero* people, which includes single-mothers, 'lost' boys and victims of abuse who have dropped out of school, work and the social mainstream.

In addition, a study published by the Children's Society in July 2006 reported that the well-being of children in Britain is amongst the lowest in Europe, undoubtedly a reflection of the size of the same *status zero* group. A report on 28 October 2006 confirmed that many of these are poor white children who perform badly at school on the assumption there seems little point if no learning is required for traditional jobs. Conversely many Asian children achieve academic standards but then fail to build a private sector career and seek security in public service. Others tend to qualify as professionals.

There seems little chance that the socially disadvantaged are able to find or hold down jobs in a hi-tech world where only 10% are employed in industry and in general, the service sector requires at least some academic skills. They will find it difficult to form stable relationships and the same group are probably responsible for the one-third of all pregnancies that were terminated for girls under twenty. At the same time these young women are likely to be infected by chlamydia – a sexually transmitted disease that can cause infertility unless treated.

Should the level of benefit be diminished because the state had reached the limit of its ability to tax or borrow, this would almost certainly lead to an unacceptable increase of crime such as the gang-wars in America, stabbings in Britain, riots in France and terrorist attacks by so-called 'martyrs' whom some cleric has encouraged to believe that paradise awaits those who kill innocent infidels. Some proposals on how these matters may be tackled are set out later.

Provide for the most endangered in society

An approach to increase local responsibility was initiated by President Clinton in September 1997 which encouraged a degree of innovation, the most famous being the Wisconsin Works programme (W-2) initiated by Governor Tommy Thompson. The W-2 aimed to provide welfare, employment and support to primarily unmarried mothers with children who were near poverty level and had few assets. At the outset there were certain principles:

- For those able to work, there should be no payment without work.
- Everyone is assumed able to work; at the very least, everyone is capable of contributing to society according to their abilities.
- All policies must be judged in terms of how well they strengthen parental responsibility to care for their children. This is the task of parents, not the state.
- A new system should reward work and help self-sufficiency for services that are needed.
- Private sector alternatives – as an alternative to municipal services – should be encouraged.

- Housing policy should be based on preventing homelessness and moving people into self-sustaining employment rather than proliferating shelters.

To assess the best programme for each individual there is an active aptitude and medical screening process that divides participants into three categories in ascending order of ability:

- Traditional placements provide work practice and training for those unable to sustain independent, self-sustaining work. For this there was a cash benefit of $673 monthly.
- Community service jobs which provide work experience and training for those able to perform some job duties and are expected to eventually move into unsubsidised employment. For this the monthly benefit was $628. Many of these jobs were working in schools, hospitals, healthcare offices and other community groups.
- Trial jobs provide work experience and training that may become permanent; these were unsubsidised positions capable of earning not less than the state minimum age. For this the subsidy was $300 a month.

In addition:

- Custodial parents of infants are not required to work outside the home until the child is older than 12 weeks. For this the subsidy was $673 a month.
- Client's children aged six and older were required to attend school under a Learnfare programme and there were penalties for non-attendance.

The profile of the participants fits closely the pattern of single-parent families described earlier. 60% were aged between 18 and 29, 97% were female, over half were African American and 97% reported no disability. The participants were given medical assistance and there were penalties for not reporting for duty or for their children skipping school. The programme contained the essentials for bringing people back into the mainstream including basic adult education, occupational and disability assessment, employment counselling, parenting and life skills and so on. The agencies supplying the jobs were both state and privately run and the latter were allowed to run at a profit – a proportion of which was ploughed back to the state funds.

The success of the programme was measured by the reduction of over 60% from the 81,291 families who first enrolled and the staff caseloads were down 70% while in other states it rose sharply. While this was partly due to an improving economy there were other relative benefits. The unemployment rate was lower than in other states and teen pregnancy and births at 39 per thousand was also below the national average of 59 per thousand girls. In addition the average remuneration of the client group was above the national average. The Governor of Florida also experimented with decentralised benefit and work encouragements that was adapted to suit individual needs provided they met certain goals.

In their book *The Plan*, Douglas Carswell and Daniel Hannan strongly recommend the adoption of a devolved welfare programme similar to that of W2. So help has gone a full circle from devolvement to the church wardens in early 1600s to the state run Victorian workhouses and now back to its local roots. The Plan also advocates the reintroduction of Friendly Societies, self-funding groups started by an Act of Parliament in 1793 to help working families through difficult times; they were terminated by Lloyd George in 1911. There are also many charities such as the Salvation Army that is the second largest provider of homes for the destitute in the UK and churches which have traditionally played a great part in the life of communities.

As a result decisions taken locally could separate deserving cases from scroungers and spend more on those deserving the most. Those who were weaned off benefit could either find a job or else join the

Conservation and Security Agency (CSA) or a system similar to the Guardian Angels – both described later. In both instances those recently released could work closely with professionals to provide a greater feedback from those living in dense neighbourhoods. Should the case-load be reduced, better quality staff could be afforded by the authorities.

There is also a history. Before the welfare state, a complex network of private support services existed in most American and British cities. These were provided by churches, local communities, secular societies and the like; Murray shows that in 1900, the level of voluntary support in New York far exceeded anything that the city could have provided from its official resources. Since the welfare state, many of the same societies then formed pressure groups to lobby for their favourite cause. Should the state be less active most of these would regain their former function and probably also attract many more funds.

This return to local action has been taken up by the Centre of Policy Studies in London; another report shows that the number of individuals working for voluntary organisations in Britain is eleven and a half million. This and other surveys suggest that devolving responsibility in the US had the effect of charities organising work in return for benefits and encouraging people to take job offers. It also created a spirit of inter-state competition that reduced those families on benefit from five to two million, It reduced children in poverty by 1.6 million (that included an unprecedented fall in black children in poverty by a third) and single mothers by over 15%. The report cited benefits of localisation:

- Large centralised bureaucracies are obliged to work to rules that are bound to create loopholes that permit state scroungers. This is less possible in a localised system where these individuals – and those that are more deserving – are more likely to be known.
- As in the US, pluralism provides the opportunity to experiment from which the best models can be chosen elsewhere.

- Publicly funded bodies must be morally neutral but this would not be present in, for example, a church-based society that would feel obliged to connect in a more direct fashion and attack the cause of the problem while also dealing with the symptoms. In a society that is wearying of the lack of self-discipline, maybe this is not a bad thing anyway?

- One has also to be aware that any ambitious public sector worker is bound to put the well-being and integrity of the department as their first concern. This is evident when any failures in the social service are tidily put aside in an enquiry and few are fired.

In addition many voluntary agencies are usually frugally managed to attract volunteers and donations; by their nature they can improvise in the great tradition in most English-speaking countries. A shining example is the Salvation Army, a Christian-based organisation started by William Booth in in the year 1865. It is now working in 111 countries with 1.6 million active agents.

Booth identified his mission as a spiritual war on deprivation and evil and created a persona with associated commissioned officers, uniforms, flags and bands, with women having equal status with men. Astonishingly for a privately funded organisation, Salvationists provide the second largest service after the British government in meeting the needs of homeless people through such services as soup runs, breakfast clubs, support groups, provision of food and clothing, washing facilities and advice. It does this though church and community centres, residential homes for displaced families, children's homes and residential places for the elderly and those with special needs.

The sums necessary to provide such a service are considerable. For example, in America the operating income at the turn of the century was just over $3 billion of which a third came from contributions, 11% from donations in kind, over a fifth from transferred income and some 11% from the government. Of the expenditure, only 12% went on management and general expenses (compared to 30% of most government-run services) while the majority was spent on community centres, rehabilitation services and social help. One can only wonder what such an organisation could do if it had the resources presently spent by the state in many countries!

There is also the question of transfer payments for the indigent and those who have made no provision for their old age. As explained earlier, Murray suggests that everyone over the age of 21, regardless of means, should receive a payment of $10,000 a year that would be free of tax until the total income reaches $25,000, when a 20% taxable is payable on the grant up to a limit of $2,500 up to a combined income of $50,000. From this individuals would be obliged to have this paid directly into health insurance, pension contributions, unemployment benefit and the like.

Murray argues that a state pension only pays some 2% on contributions which, if put into funds over a 45 year working life, would yield at least 4%. Should the individual be unable to provide at all for themselves, then a considerable proportion of that income would be payable for a place in Salvation Army type of accommodation.

This programme would greatly reduce the cost of administration and would eliminate all transfer payments and the organisation that supports them.

Simplify the role of Government

So far in this chapter, there would seem little need for a government department to meet the needs of health (except public health against epidemics), education, pensions, social security, welfare and related services. Unsurprisingly, what is left fits in admirably with the portfolios of the Swiss Government that has derived a very Digital Age approach towards decentralisation.

The Swiss constitution was established in 1848, the same year there were revolutions in a number of European states, in a decade that was to become known as the 'hungry forties'. In that year the cantons, of which there are now 26, ceded security, defence, economic management and foreign affairs to a Federal Council elected from a Federal Assembly, the lower house is elected by universal franchise. There is an upper house, The Council of States, elected on the basis of one or two from each canton depending upon their size. There is also a Supreme Court.

The country is managed by the Federal Council which is elected for four years and consists of seven members whose portfolios range from transport, foreign affairs, home affairs, economic management, security and defence, justice and the police, finance and the chancellery. The president is elected from one of the members, and the position rotates every year. There are also twelve sub-committees, only two of which are concerned with education or social security, who meet for three days a quarter.

The Swiss Government has operated a budget surplus since 2006 with an expenditure of around 35% of GDP. The frugality extends to the two hundred members of the National Council who are elected for four years and are required to meet four times a year for two or three week periods. The representatives do not receive a salary but can claim expenses for their periods of service. Unlike most Western countries there is an admirable system of referenda where ten thousand citizens can sign a petition to change the law that the Federal Assembly is obliged to debate, and if necessary, challenge the proposal.

It might be argued that what works for a small country of eight million people, does not necessarily apply to a larger country, but by decentralisation, the present government expenditure could be drastically reduced by obliging it to unwind responsibilities as suggested earlier without individuals being penalised.

The Swiss work on the fundamental principle that it is individuals that drive a country, not the government; secondly that Switzerland is a country whose federation has grown from the bottom up whereas in many other nations the state has taken over more and more responsibilities that could perfectly well have been left to the voluntary or private sector. The management and contribution of the Swiss army to the Digital Paradigm is described in a later chapter.

Taxation

Taxation in Switzerland is much simplified compared with most Western States, for over one third is levied from value added tax, just less than a quarter from direct federal income tax and the balance from duties on fuel, imports, tobacco and so on. Their success is shown by their ranking six in the world for per capita GDP. How then can other Western countries simplify and reduce their own tax burden? Several principles have been suggested.

The idea of a *Negative Income tax* was originally attributed to Nobel laureate Milton Friedman who suggested that the raft of transfer payments could be simplified by simply transferring cash to those below a certain income. So good did this system seem that during the 1970s the federal government sponsored a series of tests in Pennsylvania and in two cities.

The results were disappointing because all those below the set threshold had little incentive to work, particularly among the young; it also seemed to coincide with a higher rate of marital breakdowns – not dissimilar to the conditions described earlier when people do not have to work to get paid. It was this experiment that caused Charles Murray to suggest the outright payment to every citizen over the age of twenty-one to cover the essentials of health and pensions.

Patricia Morgan in her book *War Between the State and the Family* argues that there should be tax-breaks for married couples. She believes marriage should be rewarded by making couples more eligible for public housing and suggests applying strict rules for single parents and for child support. The Wisconsin W-2 project demands penalties by reduced payments for adults who do not attend the make-work programmes and for children who do not attend school.

A more recent report has been published by Lord Forsyth who suggests a much more simple system with only two basic tax bands of

20% and 40%; the lower rate being an incentive for individuals to work harder. In the place of the unpopular estate duty Forsyth suggest its abolition but requires the legatees to pay 40% on any capital gains realised. The same principle applies to encouraging new businesses. Forsyth does not set about reducing the size of government to Swiss proportions but these ideas would help the possibility.

Part 3 Chapter 2.
Valuing the Individual in Society

Summary

The purpose of this chapter is to propose how individuals could once again acquire a skill that was valuable to others. It also suggests that instead of transfer payments for people to remain idle, money should now be used for training them for the digital era. It is complementary to that of bringing the government into the Digital Age for it describes how the worst aspects of the now unaffordable industrial era, and the welfare state, may be corrected using well-tried methods. Its primary role is to lessen the dependency culture that has created an underclass and revive the tradition – still powerful in many countries in the West – of a healthy voluntary sector. This will have to deal not just with unemployment, but also the chance to create a new spirit of purpose, particularly among young people. This is in contrast to a rootless life, a drift into crime, the likelihood of rising racial tensions in difficult times and the prospect of swelling already crowded prisons.

Introduction

By the first half of 2015 it is evident that few politicians have the slightest idea of what to do about the situation set out earlier except in general terms; neither do they understand the advent of the Digital Age and the prospect of rising unemployment. At the same time, the ability of the state to underwrite idleness is rapidly diminishing so alternatives must be found. In addition, the numbers of people without regular employment in the transition could have risen to levels of perhaps a third of the working population – something quite unacceptable in a modern society with the associated crime for those with idle hands. Furthermore, there will be many who would traditionally have thought of retirement who will be without adequate support and will need additional income. Altogether any programme will probably need to incorporate some third of the population until a new equilibrium will be found.

This chapter sets out the background to any support programme and suggests how this may be implemented at minimum cost.

The human cost of the welfare state

A study in April 2007 by The London School of Economics showed there were 1.2 million people in Britain who are what they called Neets (not in education, employment or training) – twice that of Germany; to this the downwave will probably add another million unfortunates. The report estimated that this cost the taxpayer £3.65 billion a year to which a further report from the Royal Bank of Scotland adds £1 billion for the cost of crime and £18 billion for a lifetime of lost earnings. In all, the lack of political initiative is costing the taxpayer £20 billion in 2007 which would be well over £30 billion by 2015.

An earlier part showed that this figure should include between two and three million children (between 10 and 15% of homes) living in houses without anyone being in work – something that could only increase as any downturn deepens. There are also around over three million claiming disability allowances. Quite apart from the welfare state being progressively unable to support them as government revenues decline, there is the human cost to the nation of up to 10% of the population being debarred from making any contribution.

These people whom politicians have 'swept under the table' as being too difficult to deal with can be just accommodated in economical good times through transfer payments and policing. But with a major downturn, these unfortunates could be left to their own devices leading to an unacceptable increase of crime such as gang-wars in America, stabbings in Britain and riots in France. Without a sense of guidance some of the least advantaged could become radicalised to make terrorist attacks on a society that has chosen not to listen – this is quite apart from so-called 'martyrs' whom some cleric has persuaded that paradise awaits those who kill innocent infidels.

This potential employment time-bomb is not singular to Britain, it is bound to hit all westernised countries where a radical decline in the prospect of producing such commoditised products as cars, computers and other manufactured goods will generate levels of unemployment not seen for eighty or so years.

How to navigate a large minority of the population through an extremely difficult period which will see differentials of income widen dramatically is today's problem and a new opportunity to value the individual.

Employing those out of work stems back at least to Ancient Egypt when farmers, unable to till their land while the Nile flooded, were put to work building pyramids and temples. While the skilled building and fashioning work was done by masons, engravers, plasterers and painters, the humping was an unskilled task relegated to the farmers. The manhandling work on the tombs and monuments stopped when the river subsided and it was time to plant seed once again.

A similar principle was adopted early in the 13th century when the great cathedrals were built in Britain, France and Italy. When there was adequate rainfall and the crops could be expected to yield a good harvest, the farmers were recruited to handle the heavy work. Remarkably for the period, Salisbury Cathedral was built over some thirty-five years in a period of good growing weather. Building slowed in the early decades of the next century when poor weather required the farmers to till even the poorer land. It virtually stopped during the black death twenty years later to be revived later with the much plainer Perpendicular Gothic.

Two hundred years on, the first Poor Laws were passed in England in 1597/8 and 1601 to help those made destitute by the appalling weather when the population had just recovered to the same level as before the '*great dying*' – as the black death was known. The responsibility to organise help was delegated to the church wardens who were required to house and put the destitute to work in the fields while apprenticeships were found for the children.

So successful was this programme that it was copied in many other countries. It continued to be a charitable issue until 1834 when the cost of support was so great that stringent admission requirements were introduced to admit only the demonstrably needy to the workhouses.

Although the Industrial Revolution created many jobs there was a major work hiatus late in the 19th century when industrialisation took place over a generation in Germany – compared to four generations in Britain. Fearing civil unrest Otto von Bismarck, the Chancellor, introduced a mild form of the welfare state to provide help for those who suffered the most. His ideas were taken up and expanded by Lloyd George of the old Liberal government in Britain in the early 20th century; this process curtailed many charitable organisations.

The next serious attempts to alleviate unemployment were made during the 1930s in Germany and America for very different reasons: in the former, as a prelude to rearmament; in the latter as a make-work programme to deal with jobless figures of 25%. It is worth examining these to help formulate future plans.

Italy and Germany

When Mussolini became the Italian dictator in 1922 he seemed initially quite tolerant of industrialists – while they still paid their taxes – and spent money on the infrastructure such as roads and building sport stadiums; these were good times of full employment. All this changed in the early 1930s when, in an effort to reduce people being laid off, he organised a state holding company that bought into failing companies. His task was helped by re-armament for his adventures in Africa and the Balkans.

By contrast, when Adolf Hitler became Chancellor, the country's unemployment was six million, the economy was stagnant, banks had failed and many feared a communist revolution. Some two years later, the jobless total was around six hundred thousand, economic output was at pre-slump figures and inflation had been contained.

This remarkable performance, which surpassed anything achieved or that would have been acceptable in a democracy, was due to several basic principles. Among them were the Nazi election pledges to build a road infrastructure, to make Germany as self-sufficient as possible in food and a requirement to make people physically fit after a period of inaction.

All this was made possible by a ruthless programme of eliminating trade unions and political opposition, introducing financial controls that funded work programmes without inflation and a rigid fascist control of every element of society. There was, of course, a downside. Prices and wages were rigidly controlled, individuals were not allowed to leave the land for better pay elsewhere and enterprise was severely directed towards state objectives.

While this was going on the Mark was kept steady by strictly controlling foreign exchange for essential raw materials. To help keep the Mark stable, bi-lateral deals were negotiated with countries like Romania exchanging oil for manufactured items, and research was initiated to produce synthetic oil and rubber from coal. Later when Roosevelt criticised Hitler for re-armament, the Fuhrer retorted reasonably that his remedial programme had been infinitely more successful than that of the US.

The United States

In March 1933 the new president Franklin D Roosevelt's first task was to halt bank failures by calling a 'holiday'; his next act would prove to be inspired. On 21 March he sent to Congress the following proposal:

A Civilian Conservation Corps (CCC) that would be used in simple work, not interfering with normal employment, and confining itself to forestry, the prevention of soil erosion, flood control and similar projects. More important however than the material gains will be the moral and spiritual value of such work. The Americans who are now walking the streets and receiving private and public relief would infinitely prefer to work. We can take a vast army of unemployed out in to healthy surroundings. We eliminate, to some extent, the threat that enforced idleness brings to spiritual and moral stability. It is not a panacea but I estimate that 250,000 men can be given temporary employment by the early summer if you will give me the authority to proceed within the next two weeks.

He got it by 31 March.

The countryman in him told him there was clearly useful work to be done by some of the five million unemployed young men in the millions of farmland acres being eroded. In addition, huge areas were threatened by fire, and regions like the Shenandoah Hills were being made barren by indiscriminate logging for fuel. Instead of creating a new ministry, he set up an advisory council directed by Robert Fechner, a labour leader from Boston, that included representatives from the departments of Defense, Agriculture and the Interior. The idea was to open camps to be run by the armed services and the work to be supervised and training given by 'local experienced men' (LEMs).

The initial call was for 240,000 unmarried young men between the ages of eighteen and twenty-five, who had completed eight years of schooling and were from families on relief. The first call was not well supported but, after clearing away bureaucratic hurdles, 275,000 young men and First World War veterans had been recruited. Individuals were to be paid $30 a month, of which $22 was to be sent home, and there were bonus payments of up to $5 for undertaking special duties such as leading gangs, working in the cookhouse and so on. The first task was to send the volunteers to special camps where they underwent two or three weeks of nutritional and physical conditioning before they were fit enough to work.

By September 1935, enrolment had peaked at over 500,000, the recruits serving in over 2,500 camps and by 1938 over two million men had served. Once the pattern had been set, Fechner introduced education and training into the curriculum and reduced the lower age limit to seventeen.

The results were impressive: nearly 90,000 miles of telephone lines had been rigged, almost 3,500 fire towers built, more than six million days were spent fighting fires, and nearly 70,000 miles of fire-breaks dug. Other work included planting more than two billion trees, building flood protection, making footpaths, restoring woodland and forests, aiding soil conservation, working in disaster relief and restoring historic areas such as battlefields. This work was not without danger; although sound training was given, twenty-nine men died fighting fires, ten of them in Wyoming.

The CCC did not just help young men do worthwhile work, it also gradually increased the educational content as many men had dropped out of school. From 1934, an education advisor was authorised for each camp and local teachers were enlisted as volunteers to help 40,000 who could not read or write. Much of the training was vocational, such as car and truck maintenance, forestry, the handling of heavy equipment, carpentry, welding, the use of radios and so on. In addition people could study subjects such as journalism, surveying, photography and psychology, backed up by correspondence courses. When war was declared, the CCC turned over most of its camps to the army and the programme was disbanded in mid-1942 – after providing some nine years of valuable service. They also helped to reduce crime; a judge commented that the CCC was largely responsible for a 55% reduction of crime by young men in Chicago.

The CCC was the most successful programme of the New Deal but there were others such as the Work Programme Administration

(WPA) as a means of creating work for men who would otherwise be on the dole. Like the CCC, the work should not conflict with commercial operations and only one member of a family was allowed to take part. Although the WPA got a name for digging holes in the ground then filling them up again it did succeed in building, renovating, tidying-up or repairing 20,000 public areas such as playgrounds, hospitals, schools and airfields. In doing this it achieved its aim of providing people with much greater satisfaction, but the programme was not continuous and, unlike the CCC, it lacked incentives for taking more responsibility or learning additional skills.

Britain

The 1931 coalition government generated a business-friendly environment that created boom conditions in the Midlands and South East but no job creation programmes to help the deprived areas. There was major hardship among the staple industries of coal, iron, shipbuilding and textiles in outlying regions, and that generated its own unhappy legacy.

During The Second World War Britain introduced several potent quasi-voluntary organisations that could be useful guides in the present. The first was the Royal Observer Corps who manned visual aircraft spotting observation points around the coast and inland as a back-up to the Chain Home radar stations in case these were bombed or jammed. Next there were the Air Raid Wardens who were trained to guard public buildings such as St Paul's against incendiary bombs, to spot breaches in the black-out, to put out fires and to help bring people to safety.

Probably the most interesting was the Home Guard set up by Winston Churchill after the evacuation from Dunkirk in 1940. Originally armed with nothing more than pitchforks and shotguns, this gradually became a properly armed and trained force acting as a back-up to the army in case of invasion. They knew their locality, guarded essential buildings, bridges, power stations and so on. Some were trained as a fifth column in case of enemy occupation.

Ingredients for a latter-day employment and welfare programme

We can now identify the programmes that meet the needs set out earlier and policies that work and those that do not. History brought up to date shows us what should be done:

- Individuals working either singly or in groups bring a democratic economy out of recession, not the state; the best politicians can do is to create a stable currency, cut any restrictions to enterprise and provide protection, where necessary, from imports dumped from abroad.
- Any recovery should include a spiritual element confirming the belief that individuals would be much better working constructively than being idle. In the early decades of the 21st century any programme must include defence against religious terrorism.
- The concept of the CCC should be a model for any new make-work plan. At its lowest level it should provide useful work for relatively simple but necessary local tasks, reward for responsibility and skills, remedial education and any promotional services. Experience shows it would help to reduce violence, truancy, and act as a back-up for dysfunctional families. Part of the programme should help to bring *status zero* people and children back into the mainstream – their existence is an indictment on the state, the churches and society.
- A modern CCC could use an organisation such as the Guardian Angels – described later – to help the police and security services to guard against terrorist attacks, patrolling school grounds against marauders and drug dealers, helping to reduce violence on the

streets and transport and acting as vigilantes as a support for law enforcement.

- The educational element is important for much of employment creation will be for self-employment.
- At the national level there will be an increasing need for individuals to be trained in disaster relief from incidents such as earthquakes, flooding, tsunamis, refugees and so on. This might be a semi-military force, along the lines of the Swiss citizens army described later. Many of these individuals could later join the armed forces if the need for military support increases.
- The local programmes should be managed by voluntary organisations and paid with funds normally set aside as unemployment or incapacity benefit. In addition there would be revenue from work done by individuals and groups contracting these services – see TCV below.
- National programmes should be managed by the military personnel.
- The German experience taught the importance of individual health and fitness.
- Welfare programmes for those not immediately absorbed by work-creation programmes should be decentralised and administered locally just as the first Poor Laws were administered in the Late Elizabethan period and Wisconsin's W-2 described earlier.
- Any programmes should have the effect of reducing crime as was the experience of the CCC.
- Anyone can leave the programme for gainful work.

The policies that do not work:
- Paying for people to do nothing. This includes those suffering from a range of disabilities, single parents and those apparently looking for work, see the W-2 initiative.

- One-off work generating plans described later do not fulfil the need. The New Deal's Public Works Administration (PWA) was excellent for achieving big project benefits to the infrastructure but employed relatively few people. Japan emulated Roosevelt's New Deal in the 1990s and succeeding in building roads and railways that led nowhere which generated a large budget deficit, big borrowings but were no cure for unemployment.

The next sections suggest how a *Latter-Day CCC* could probably be grafted on to existing voluntary organisations at local and national level. Among these examples are the National Trust, the Conservation Volunteers in the UK, the Guardian Angels, the Defense 2eme Chance in France and the Swiss Army. At some level it would be sensible for national programmes to be managed by the armed forces who, by their nature, are skilled at training and organising large numbers of people. All these, in their own ways, could help to meet the objectives set out earlier.

The National Trust (NT)

The NT was founded in 1895 to 'preserve places of historic interest or natural beauty permanently for the nation to enjoy'. Being independent of the government it relies on the generosity of its supporters through membership subscriptions, gifts, legacies and the contribution of over 35,000 volunteers. It charges for admission and owns around 612,000 acres of the most beautiful countryside and almost 600 miles of coastline. It has in its care over 200 historic houses and gardens and nearly fifty industrial monuments and mills.

While all the managing staff are salaried, there are a large number of opportunities for volunteers. For example, in the Thames and Solent region there are clerical openings in the departments of fund-raising, marketing, education, exhibitions, historic building guides and box-office staff that can absorb talents of all ages and abilities and disabilities.

Before joining, volunteers receive an induction programme which includes such matters as the role of the NT, health, safety and first aid. The remainder of the training is working alongside professional staff before becoming fully-fledged. There are, however, openings for long-term volunteers who contract to give twenty-one hours a week for at least three months. These may be undergraduates wishing to complement their own specialisations with practical and supervised work.

The Conservation Volunteers (TCV)

The TCV was set-up in the 1950s as a Conservation Corps that was expanded in the 1960s to include education and training. The idea was developed in the 1970s by opening offices around the mainland and it became TCV with a head office in Doncaster, Yorkshire.

Unlike the NT, TCV is obliged to charge for its services and its clients are widespread; among them are farmers, councils, local or national park supervisors, schools, the Ministry of Defence and commercial organisations. A project is initiated when a potential client calls upon someone in a local office (150 in nine regions). It is then assessed whether it is suitable for volunteers and if so, the job is costed. If the proposal is accepted it will be scheduled either locally or nationally depending upon the size and scope. Some work may require heavy equipment in which case the volunteers work alongside the contractors. Great care is taken not to engage in work that might otherwise be undertaken commercially.

Like the CCC, TCV has a spiritual element of inspiring people to enjoy transforming places that might otherwise go untended and improving the lives of those living in devastated areas of inner cities. It also aims to enrich the lives of over a million people by providing voluntary opportunities that will improve their health and education.

Most of the projects are countryside and environmentally-based, such as planting trees, clearing overgrown woodland, maintaining national parks and nature reserves. Among urban projects was one in

Lambeth, London where volunteers worked to clear a distressed site, levelled it, planted trees and constructed gardens and playgrounds; the maintenance has now been taken over by the residents. Other city work includes working within communities to help relationships, reducing drug-taking and violence, cleaning up the streets and improving citizenship. Up to 40% of the urban projects are engaged in clearing waste land and canals, planting trees, repairing buildings and so on.

More recently TCV has established overseas links with similar organisations. In the year ending they organised seventy holidays in twenty-three countries including Kenya and Gambia; in the former, volunteers supported the Colobus Trust helping to conserve endangered primates. This activity is growing and there are plans for further linkages.

The Guardian Angels

The Guardian Angels were set up by Curtis Silwa in 1979. Silwa was the manager of the East Fordham Road McDonald's in New York frequented by many Puerto Rican youths. He originally set out to clean up garbage in the street then later to combat the widespread violence and crime in the city's subways. Its members, dressed in T-shirts, red jackets and berets, were trained to make citizen's arrests – action that attracted public praise and official criticism, who accused them of being naïve vigilantes causing more trouble than good.

The Angels action precipitated a deep social and political debate about the role of government and the citizen in society and in due course led to moves by the authorities to involve people more closely in their communities. This led to the Angels improving their training with an emphasis on safety that led to better relations with the police and by the mid-1990s Mayor Rudolph Guiliani had become their most loyal supporter.

By the new century the Angels were running Safety Patrols, walking the streets or riding on public transport and, by encouraging people to become more involved, to help to make streets safer. Although they can make citizens arrests, their main focus is to deter crime and drug-dealing and their work has led them to schools where they help teachers deal with unruly behaviour, patrol playgrounds, deter bullies and keep watch over entrances. In addition the CyberAngels have been initiated to track down paedophiles, educate children and parents and set out safety rules for the vulnerable of the 205 million Americans who regularly use the internet.

The organisation is now run by Mary Silwa, an executive with a proven managerial record, who is concentrating on increasing professionalism, fund-raising, training and integrating the group both into society, and with the authorities. The Angels recruit from a wide range of age, ethnic and social backgrounds and there is a screening process that excludes previous trouble-makers. Apart from the USA, it now has 'chapters' in Japan, the United Kingdom, South Africa and Canada and has groups in some of the toughest cities in the world.

Defense 2eme Chance

This is an imaginative initiative launched by the French prime minister in September 2005 with the objective of helping young people to become active and useful citizens. Not unlike the CCC, it was launched in conjunction with the ministries of Defense and the Interior, and the first centre was opened at Monty in the Departement of Seine-et-Marne on 30 September 2005.

Each year 800,000 young French people participate in the Journee d'Appel of which 60,000 are experiencing learning difficulties and 20,000 could be classified in the *status zero* category mentioned earlier. The aim is to engage with this lowest group by taking volunteers from young people in the age group of 18 to 21 for a period that can last from six months to two years. They wear uniforms.

The first six months are spent in remedial work, both physical and educational, to bring them up to a general standard of competence with a routine similar to that of young soldiers. The next six months they are taught a vocational skill in such areas as the hotel trade, personnel services, security, maintenance or in the building trade. It is planned to open two more centres. This is an excellent programme that satisfies some of the main criteria of what is needed, such as helping to make young people into healthy and useful citizens with a working education. However, unlike the CCC, it lacks continuity of dealing with unemployment which, at around 25%, is particularly high among the under 25s in France,.

The Swiss Army

The Swiss Army is a unique force that emerged from the history of the republic when, in 1848, the defence of the country was ceded by the cantons to become a federal responsibility. By law, each person between the ages of 18 and 30 is obliged to undergo military training – although there are a number of exceptions through ill-health, education or reluctance to bear arms. This implies that there are over one and a half million potential recruits, the second largest per capita force after Israel. The size of the army is now 220,000 including reservists. There are 3,600 professional staff.

There is an initial training period of eighteen to twenty-one weeks depending on the branch of service when the recruits learn the rudiments of soldiery and are able to use the standard Sig 500 rifle, the Sig automatic pistol and a Stinger hand-held anti-aircraft missile. There are then annual regular range training and equipment checks. All service men and women keep their rifles at home and are issued with a sealed box of fifty rounds for self-defence in case of emergency while joining their units. Remarkably, full mobilisation can be achieved in twelve hours – compared with months for the United States National Guard. This has only been ordered three times in relatively modern times: in 1870, and during two world wars.

There are penalties for not joining up. The dissidents are obliged to pay an additional 3% on their income tax and serve in Civil Protection which can mean the police, fire department, social service, environmental work, helping the elderly and so on. They also have to spend 50% more time than their military colleagues.

S4Y – Soldiers for Youth

S4Y is an imaginative programme initiated by Wandsworth Council in conjunction with John Lawton, a philanthropist. The idea is to recruit ex-soldiers to work either as volunteers or salaried to work with young people in the London Borough. A successful programme has obvious extensions to other inner-cities.

In Summary

We now have a pattern of past and present working ingredients for proposals some of which meet the objectives set out earlier.

- The Defense 2eme Chance is a methodical vocational training service which is an excellent initiative working within an age group; it probably lacks continuity for individuals as they get older, but should fit into a larger and continuous programme such as NRA described below.
- The example of the W-2, described earlier, Britain's wartime volunteers and the Swiss Army have the virtue of being continuous and should form part of the overall plan.
- The National Trust and TCV already exist to provide work, training and any programme should be grafted on to their work.
- The CCC provides an excellent template for dealing with a very large problem but there should be no age limit.

It is of interest that no official organisation trains for self-employment! There should be opportunities to move in and out of the programme.

Let us call the new organisation...

The Conservation and Security Agency (CSA)

This proposed organisation is designed to put to work the unemployed and disabled (whose numbers are above 6% of those of working age in the UK); in fact anyone who wants to claim benefit or who might be sent to do community service. As a matter of principle it should make the maximum use of those of pensionable age who would wish to increase their income to act either as participants or instructors – just as did the LEMs in the CCC. It would have the secondary objective of giving fundamental skills to those left behind by the state education system and to prepare those who want to become self-employed. The participants can leave at any time for employment when their support will stop. There will be no pay without work.

Putting the unemployed to work

This must form part of any programme aimed to effect the transfer to the Digital Age where many individuals will feel displaced and need retraining. It should also aim to attract individuals such as volunteers who would want to pass on their skills by acting as trainers, supervisors or participants. Its task would be to enrol and give training to all that were claiming state benefit except those with children up to twelve weeks – see W-2 programme. After initial aptitude and medical screening tests, individuals would be guided into three levels of participation:

- Local projects connected with the environment, needy people and helping with security.
- National disaster relief and helping with infrastructure projects.
- Quasi-military and overseas disaster relief.

Local projects

These imply that the individuals would live locally and could expect to go home after a day's work. They would be managed by the local council and paid a flat rate but there would be additions for taking responsibility, specialist training such as disease containment, dangerous work or for particular tasks. Where possible they would be seconded to organisations such as the National Trust, TCV or The Angels. Otherwise, their work would include:

- Helping with county-based organisations involved in preserving heritage by tending sites that are of ecclesiastical, military, industrial, historical, environmental and other interest.
- To support the authorities in their measures to contain pandemics such as helping to bring essentials to those most affected.
- To expand the work of the TCV-style projects into many rural and urban areas.
- In conjunction with the police, provide Guardian Angel type patrols on public transport, playgrounds, schools, drug-ridden or violent streets and so on. They would be connected to the police radio networks.
- To assist old people with tasks such as shopping, home decorating and possibly companionship.
- To support the National Recovery Agency (NRA) – set out later – through organising crèches, helping manage the units and so on.
- To form local intelligence either openly or through the internet on the lines of Vigil in the UK and others in the US that help to increase national security, unearth paedophiles, uncover terrorist plots or reveal those plotting crimes.
- Time would be made available, where necessary, for remedial writing, maths and basic subjects.

- There would be on offer specific training for trades and self-employment and there would be many occasions where those of pensionable age could help with vocational training.

Like the CCC the participants may need conditioning to bring them up to a standard of fitness and would wear a uniform on active duty. They would be paid weekly by the employing organisation who could also claim a training allowance that various governments spend on varying degrees from 0.5% of GDP up to 1.8%; there would be deductions for poor behaviour, timekeeping or slacking. They could also reward merit and for taking responsibility.

National Disaster Relief

This would raise the level of work to the national tasks undertaken by the CCC. They could live away from home and be specially trained, supervised and paid for national disaster relief; they would be organised by the armed services. Their work would include:

- Taking action to prevent fires by digging fire-breaks, clearing undergrowth and so on. They might also support the fire brigade in firefighting.
- Reviving national networks such as canals, railways, paths or bridleways.
- Flood relief.
- Assisting the authorities with disasters including giving first aid, repairing buildings and levees, clearing rubble, establishing water or electricity supplies, creating sites for the survivors and so on.

They too would wear uniform and be paid a premium for their skills and risks. In addition to receiving specific vocational training, there would be the opportunity for a much wider academic syllabus.

International Relief

This could become the quasi-military counterpoint to the Swiss Army described earlier. They would undertake basic military and extensive training in disaster relief and be available for peace-keeping duties now undertaken by the regular or auxiliary armies; for this they would be under military discipline.

At times they could be merged with the National Disaster Group. However, their primary role would be to help with earthquakes, tsunamis, major flooding and assisting with resettling refugees such as those in Darfur. This would form a useful training ground for the regular armed forces.

Funding – some additions

Apart from the normal unemployment benefit there would be extras for TCV type of work and where local groups would wish to reward the work done. They could employ barter-style payments such as those offered by the Local Exchange Trading system (LETS) first started in British Columbia by Michael Linton.

The original LETS worked with a currency that Linton called a 'green dollar'. The providers included such services as domestic help, provision of food and clothing, baby-sitting, building, gardening and interior design; all these are recorded in a directory that is widely circulated. When work is required the buyer contacts an individual providing the service and the fee is agreed; once done a transaction note is completed and the provider credited with the fee less a small percentage for running the system. The credit can now be spent within others in the directory. Latterly more business-style work has been added such as transport, office work, language and translation services and so on.

A practical example of how 'time dollar' tokens might be used is given by a social health organisation called Elderplan in Brooklyn that is supported by local firms that offered to take the tokens. This project pays credits to over a thousand volunteers who work helping old people with shopping, home decoration, taking them to surgeries, organising self-help groups and caring for the bereaved. The programme has the public backing from politicians, and local authorities.

The CSA takes account of society's needs to protect itself, find useful work for its young people, lower crime generated through boredom or idleness and help to educate those from whom the school system has failed. There is the further group: the children from families or single people who contribute to the unacceptable pool of *status zero* children.

National Recovery Agency (NRA)

The NRA is a modern equivalent of the Elizabethan programme designed to rescue those *status zero* children and teenagers who represent such a disgraceful failure on behalf of society as a whole. Like the CCC and Defense 2eme Chance, we must look to the military to provide the ordered structure for helping youngsters back into the mainstream. There are many able people who could help:

- There are skills provided by the modern equivalent of the Local Experienced Men (LEMs) that taught the young men in the CCC. Many of these might be retired carpenters, electricians, builders, gamekeepers, farmers, ex-servicemen, countrymen, nurses, cooks and so on who could be pleased to help youngsters.
- There will be a number in the CSA programme who would have the skills to lead groups, provide abilities, help in the administration and so on.
- There is likely to be support from local sports clubs or scouts to provide regular training for activity badges.

It is likely that the work of the NRA would attract a number of people from churches, social groups, charitable organisations, local firms and the like who would be happy to assist in such a worthwhile programme. Having been considered as the underclass there are still many people who need to be helped back into society.

Introducing a local W-2-type programme described earlier, the aim would be to bring back into society those who had become left behind and with little hope of entering the constructive mainstream and meet certain goals. The W-2 is also strongly recommended by Douglas Carswell and Daniel Hannan in *The Plan*.

Self-employment

Self-employment could be an attractive alternative for those not in full-time work or in the CSA and one in tune with the Digital Age. The tradition of working for oneself used to be strong until the growth of the industrial age and is still pursued among Chinese and Indian migrants who generally score good grades in education. Many aspirants, however, get put off by the failure-rate for small businesses which is as high as 75% in the US over three years from start-up. One way of raising the success-rate is to copy an existing business though franchising.

One such is the Texan Dwyer Group that was started by Don Dwyer in 1980. The first venture was a carpet cleaning and dyeing business that, after a successful pilot scheme, generated a number of franchisees. The idea is that the franchisor creates a successful business that can be replicated through a format able to be copied by others. The franchisor provides the business plan and support operation, the franchisee learns the business for a fee then pays a royalty on sales once up and running.

The Dwyer Group believes in the principle of 'multiplication' whereby their franchisees are offered different products to be sold to the same customers. For example, the portfolio includes a drain-cleaning and plumbing service, a refurbisher of bathroom fittings and a Mr Electric franchise. This is a maintenance plan that has been nominated by the makers of ceiling fans, indoor and outdoor lighting, current-surge protectors and service-panel installations and upgrades. There is a franchise fee and the royalty on sales varies between three and six per cent depending on volume. Apart from working for themselves, Dwyer offer a business person a package whereby they can manage several individuals working as employees.

There are already many franchises offered by the *International Franchise Organisation Handbook* but also the possibility that many other different and innovative business could be franchised. One such list has been drawn up the Local Enterprise Agency of Newcastle-on-Tyne which has created Business Opportunity Profiles of some two hundred new activities – many of which might be franchised. There are clear opportunities for an investor to sponsor the replication of a successful small business through franchising at home and internationally.

Part 3 Chapter 3.
Adapting the Individual to the Digital Age

Introduction

The individual will be the biggest winner and heaviest loser in the passage through the very difficult time described in other chapters. The winners will be the top 5% able to see advantage in any diversity to create new entities, ideas and opportunities. There will also be the large minority – among them previously well-paid managers and civil servants – who will be obliged to enrol in the CSA described earlier.

Also, unlike the industrial era where there were many big companies providing a career ladder for many, in future the enterprises are likely to be technically based (see Part 5), although much smaller than at present, and some unlikely to be long-lasting. This will create many specialists able to rent their services to non-competitive principals. It is a career path not only for professionals but also for the para-professionals who will have major roles to play as intermediaries.

This manual has also emphasised the growth in power, accomplishment and importance of the individual not just in economic but also in political and social terms with a much more fluid society. Where once a person could only air their ideas politically either directly or through the media, the internet has provided a platform for many people to vote on many issues, provide information, ideas or their services in a way unimagined by previous generations.

This new sense of liberty is one of the central themes of this manual which examines how the environment of the early decades of the 21st century can bring new hope to many – irrespective of their age – who may have felt that life was over after they had been made redundant. This chapter suggests some of the new opportunities that will open up.

Opportunities

Retirement

Retiring becomes less of an option when the ability of the state to support those over 65 reduces and private pensions become less valuable through currency depletion. This presents individuals, and those employing them, with a range of opportunities to transfer accumulated knowledge and experience taking into account the older person's increasing reluctance to travel and also to tire more quickly. The previous chapters on unwinding the state will have provided many opportunities to pass on vocational and other skills to the rising level of people made redundant both through the recession and transfer to the new era.

There should also be opportunities for helping the rising number of small businesses created through franchising or the suggestion that particular niche businesses could be replicated. The franchisors will need help in writing manuals and the franchisees assistance in training, providing a back-up service, help with accounts and administration and so on.

Surprisingly, retirement homes could be centres of enterprise providing a wide range of skills to the neighbourhood and a means of helping with the fees and keeping people active. Homes could be set up with particular specialities such as legal, accounting, property, training or help with administration using modern methods of communication. Others could provide more vocational skills such as carpentry, plumbing, electrical, gardening, tailoring, cookery, nursing or help with children. The services would be locally based and could be complementary to tradesmen or small business people to help with overloads or when the principal is away on holiday.

Professional boutiques

These will become more in vogue with the advent of fewer large, and many smaller companies. These will provide a one-stop accounting, legal, property, architectural and probably other professional services. These new groups will probably also attract para-professional services set up to help small business that cannot afford professional fees.

Distance learning

Distance learning will become increasingly popular and is already in vogue by some universities offering the ability to participate in lectures remotely in interactive degree courses. It is intended that the School of Global Recovery will use this technique increasingly and offer diplomas.

Unwinding the state services

This will be a source of opportunities particularly for the para-services. Whenever the market becomes open, new niches appear. For example, one could expect para-medicals to set up first-aid boutiques open 24 hours a day to deal with small injuries and with the remit to pass onto the medical profession those patients it cannot cope with. One could envisage speciality medical practices undertaking diagnostic and out-patient operations as part of specialisations normally undertaken by hospitals.

Privatising the schools system would provide a wide range of establishments stretching from the great private and grammar schools to those offering much more practical instruction. It is likely that an extensive range of qualifications would be created acceptable to potential employers or to franchisors. Where once the local school just taught children it could become a business centre offering specialist training, remedial instruction or a venue for local classes with access to web-based distance learning centres.

Technology and innovation

Technology will become the driving force of the Digital Age – just as it did in the early part of the 18th century; then it was empirical, now it will be science-based although there will be many spin-offs just as there are at present. While much of it will be research based, engineers will be at a premium just as they were during the 1930s when innovation to create new products required every firm to attract scarce resources. As with medicine, there will be many openings for para-technicians and resources will be needed to train these individual – possible through apprenticeships.

Centres of excellence

These have been suggested earlier for new and old technologies with special tax and other advantages. These ideas could be extended to more vocational skills where centres would provide training in the latest technology, techniques and sources of financial and management support. If this was accepted internationally, there would be many opportunities for cross-fertilisation of trades and skills.

Direct selling

Direct selling will provide many openings when suppliers seek to cut out the margin of the wholesaler and retailer. In the 1990s Japanese farmers sold directly to customers. Now many will be following the lead of Avon Cosmetics when agents will be selling such items as clothes, computers and accessories, radios and the like. This could be accompanied by independent service agents.

Franchising

This is a more secure method of starting a business than most start-ups. In addition to the wide range of services already offered, franchising will be also used as finishing operations for manufacturers where added value may be had by enhancing a basic product.

Homeworking

Already in use for many professions, homeworking will increase dramatically as the ability to communicate will be such that it will enable regular meetings to be held remotely where the transferring of documents electronically will be routine. It will be used by concerns who wish to retain expertise but reduce their break-even point. Although this may be impossible for government departments to conceive at present, the need to cut central expenditure will demand higher productivity achieved either by hiving out routine functions to the private sector or to homeworkers. The greater concentration on the home will also apply to health and security where vital functions will be monitored continuously and downloaded to a home-based computer programmed to inform the local medical practice when the signals are outside limits.

Temporary working agencies

Temporary work will be an option for those either as an alternative to the make-work CSA programmes or as a chosen life-style that could become quite popular – particularly for people who wish to pursue a number of interests either inside or outside the home. It may also be an attractive way of creating a more permanent position. Already a rising number of agencies are offering this facility.

Local Exchange and Trading System (LETS)

LETS has been mentioned earlier as a simple bartering system in communities as a means of bringing together a range of abilities and services. It is this sort of system that often brings out skills that people didn't know they possessed.

Creating stepping-stones for those who have never worked

This will be an essential element of the training programme, for there will not be the funds to keep all, except those with total disabilities, in idleness; described as the NRA in Part 3 Chapter 2. This will probably take the form of one step down from the para professionals who are an essential element to a recovery. For example one step below a gardener will be someone able to tend and cut hedges, care for and mow lawns, grow vegetables, prepare and sow flower beds and so on.

The same principle could be applied to trades such as carpentry, plumbing, building, electrical services, nursing, first aid, tutoring, child care and the like; once started, there will be a large number of opportunities to broaden the base. The training will need to cover not only the skill itself but how to win business, dealing with customers and simple bookkeeping; there would be an advantage to offer many skills to the same customer. Clearly an individual will need a portfolio of skills to tide them over the seasons and there have to be opportunities for moving up the ladder to become para professionals or to widen the skill base.

Internal security

Internal security is likely to become a much more community issue with the professional police force more employed in solving crime than in local patrolling. Instead individuals can train to provide a local service such as the Guardian Angels and connect to local police forces on their radio networks.

Careers in banking and finance

These could be very different from today's working in big national organisations – few of which are unlikely to survive the severe deflationary forces hitting highly leveraged nations. Instead banking is likely to return to its 18th century roots started by wealthy individuals aiming to serve a town or county. It will be locally driven to help local enterprises, particularly those in the new taxed-advantaged enterprise zones.

Politics

If on the Swiss model described elsewhere, politics will be much more local in character with national assemblies being composed of part-time delegates with only a few full-time elected officials. These would head the great departments of state such as the treasury, internal security, maintaining the laws of the country, external defence and foreign affairs.

There will, however, be more important local assemblies than at present managing affairs that were previously the responsibility of central government and those more directly associated with people. One can imagine a wide diversity of political systems ranging from the laissez faire to even Marxist competing for votes. There would also be extensive use of consultation both at national and local level by increasing use of referenda. Like the Swiss Cantons, the region or states will compete to attract new business.

The rise of faith

This usually accompanies difficult times when people are often disorientated by rapidly changing circumstances and are attracted to beliefs and strengths outside themselves. This is a particularly important time for clerics of all denominations and faiths who will be needed to administer not only to their own flock but particularly to those who previously believed their careers and incomes were safe and have now found them ended. The disorientated will also need the voluntary sector that already plays an important part within the English-speaking peoples. A further pointer to a return to a more thoughtful period is a loose cycle of around six hundred and thirty years when the ideas of the great Greek philosopher Plato attract a rising following. We are approaching such a period now.

Part 3 Chapter 4.
An Environment Fit for Entrepreneurs

"The bureaucratisation of capitalism is killing the spirit of entrepreneurship"
Joseph Schumpeter

"Entrepreneurship... is the bold and imaginative deviator from established business patterns and practices"
Howard Stevenson

Summary

Creating the environment for entrepreneurs to thrive is one of the most important responsibilities of any politician caring for their nation's future; history shows they are the driving forces of recovery. The state needs to create stable conditions and this chapter contains some suggestions how a large minority of the population may be helped to become independent in what otherwise would be very difficult trading environment.

Introduction

Webster's New Dictionary defines what entrepreneurs do thusly: one who organises, manages, and assumes the risks of a business or enterprise. The word stems from the French *entrepreneur* meaning one who brings together. Statistically there are twice as many successful business start-ups for those aged over 50 than those of 25 and below – so clearly experience is also important.

It follows that anyone prepared to risk him- or herself must have qualities of understanding opportunities in the market place, be able to innovate, seize opportunities, lead others, be able to market, have commitment and so on. To be able to own and hold property is fundamental.

To bring it into a wider focus: the Austrian School of Economics holds that entrepreneurship is the driving force in economic development being able to constantly adapt means to ends as part of a dynamic process of discovering profit opportunities that did not exist before; it follows that once a new entity has been created it is likely to generate a whole series of further moves while the market undergoes a continuous process of readjustment.

It also follows that entrepreneurship cannot successfully exist in the rigid fascist state of the 1930s or in state direction implicit in the New Deal when big companies were favoured for funds. More recently, the regulations implicit in the EU's attempt to create a 'level playing-field' inhibits innovation and experimentation that the Austrians believe is the harmonious force of society to remove distortions.

How, then, is it possible to replicate the conditions that so enabled Britain to actually grow during the Great Depression described in this manual? The essential components are a regime of stable currency, a balanced government budget, low interest rates and taxation coupled with minimum regulation. In the Digital Age, a high proportion of the population will find themselves without a regular income, many of whom in their own way could be successful working on their own.

Essential Components

Stable Currency

A stable currency was largely achieved by Britain's devaluation by 25% after leaving the gold standard in 1931; the US administration devalued the US dollar nearly 70% against gold in 1934. Both created stability and low interest rates. The French devaluation against gold in 1928 and 1937 created anything but stability. In the 21st century it is quite possible that major currencies will once again be obliged to devalue against gold – a move that would remove the ability of politicians and central bankers to manipulate economies for political ends.

Balanced Budget

Achieving a balanced budget to allow entrepreneurs to thrive was the subject of much political debate in the early 1930s in Britain, but it was essential to allow enterprising individuals to borrow at the lowest interest rates. By 2015 most major governments are being forced to borrow extensively to meet their spending programmes which pyramids their interest payable; this is a policy failure that totally fails to learn from the past. The steps needed for politicians to unwind their present spending is described in a former chapter and needs to be coupled with a policy to regain control of the state sectors balance sheet. The Austrian School believe that innovators could find new ways of providing services that were public.

Taxation

Taxation was also a subject of much debate before the Coalition government in 1931 when the Labour cabinet split over the need to cut expenditure and so regain confidence in the pound. Greater light was shone on the level of taxation in the 1970s when Art Laffer, a professor at the University of Chicago, identified a parabola on its side shown below with government revenue on the x-axis and taxation levels on the vertical axis. Clearly when taxation is zero the state gets nothing and when a hundred percent there is no incentive to earn.

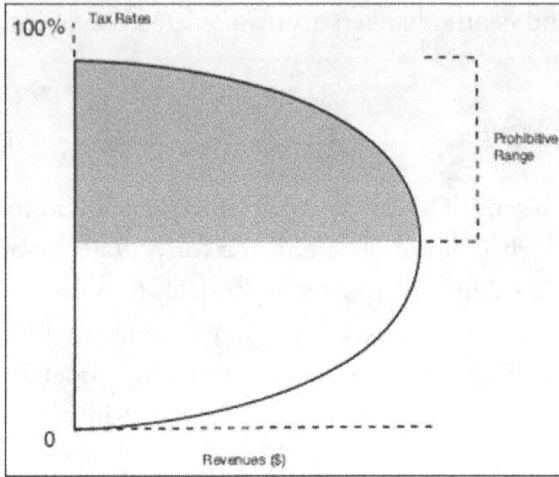

Diagram 4. The Laffer Curve

Laffer argues that the ideal zone for growth is well below the apex of the curve – remember the state take in Victorian time was around 10%. From the present position of high taxation, if tax rates are lowered the state revenue will diminish in the short term but the economic impact of individuals working harder increases the take. As the economy grows, fewer people are unemployed so that transfer payments are also diminished. The converse of what happens when taxes are raised is also true. The upper half of the curve is labelled prohibited territory because clearly higher taxes are bound to reduce revenue as individuals see no point in working hard or conceal their earnings.

In his 2004 paper Laffer cites three periods during the 20th century when the theory generated a higher GDP in the US:.

- The first occurred after the First World War when the top marginal tax rate rose to 75%; there was a sharp recession in 1920 before the Warren Harding administration cut the rate to 25%. In the three years to 1927 the government revenue was in surplus, the growth of the GDP rose from 2% to 3.4% and unemployment more than halved. To illustrate the further effect on employment, the share of those paying tax in the lowest bracket declined from 1.9 to 0.4%.

- The Roosevelt administration raised the top rate progressively to above 80% and it remained high until the Kennedy administration lowered the top rate from 91 to 70%. In the years to 1968, taxed revenue increased fourfold, there was a marginal rise in GDP and unemployment fell from 5.6% to 3.9%.

- The Reagan administration cut rates progressively from the top marginal rate of 70% (where they had remained during the deep recession of the late 1970s) down to 28% in 1988. The result was the federal deficit became a surplus, the GDP growth rose to nearly 5% and unemployment declined from 8% to 7% in 1986. In the early 1980s capital gains tax was reduced from 28% to 20% and the income rose by 50%.

The arguments advanced by Laffer put into sharp contrast the unlikely success of the tax policies being imposed on both sides of the Atlantic. During a recession wise governments will offer particular tax and regulatory advantages to retain and encourage any business setting up on their territory.

Business regulations

It is a truism that governments increase regulations long after the damage has been done and at the worst possible time to initiate recovery; as would be expected there is a negative correlation between the number of new businesses and rising regulations. Typically in the last decade, while paying lip-service to helping business, politicians have heaped barrier upon barrier to the nascent business person. The list is in testament to this total lack of understanding:

- Register with the tax authorities
- Collect tax on sales

- Collect tax and national insurance from employees for the Treasury
- Pay business rates
- Carry out detailed health and safety checks on premises even though it is your own home
- Minimise fire risk
- Ensure easy access for disabled people
- Minimise employee risk and insure staff for any ailments picked-up while working
- Register the business when working in particular sectors
- Protect data
- Prevent money laundering
- Draw up employment contracts
- Pay the minimum wage and allow holidays
- Allow minimum level of sick pay due to stress
- Paid annual leave
- Allow unpaid time off
- No discrimination due to age, sex, race or religious beliefs
- Allow for paid paternity and maternity leave
- Allow for workers disabilities
- Arrange flexible working arrangements
- Work through detailed procedures before firing an employee

All these are possibly laudable when things are going well but a terrible disincentive for the new business person when times are tough and the main consideration is to obtain a sale, fulfil it and receive payment. During the 1930s it was possible to start up many operations such as motor cars, commercial vehicles, aircraft, engines, electronic devices, domestic appliance, construction and many other businesses just applying Common Law. Any nation going back to the first principles of law and contract will find themselves at very considerable advantages when attracting entrepreneurs.

About being an entrepreneur in the Digital Age

Over the last two hundred years in the industrial era there were three depressions in the US which each produced their own new employment opportunities:

- After the depression and Mexican War of the 1840s the US acquired Texas, New Mexico, Arizona and California, all of which encouraged the '49 gold rush, growth of railroads and the great western farmlands.
- The depression of the late 1890s brought forth the mass-production of the Model T Ford through the genius of FW Taylor and there were many imitators.
- The 1930s and 40s saw Taylor's ideas extended to such areas as tanks, ships, aircraft, domestic appliances and, with the advent of the computer, to much improved production, distribution and retail management.

The Digital Age opportunities will be quite different and are unlikely to be variants of the industrial era when a high proportion of the population were engaged in manufacturing. In the future between 5 and 10% of the population are likely to be the natural entrepreneurs who will need the backing of perhaps 40%. Assuming another 15% will be needed in manufacturing, farming and government, this leaves a large minority without regular employment and, unlike the start of the industrial revolution that took place over generations, the entry into the Digital Age will occur within a working lifetime. However, many new opportunities will arise as described in earlier chapters.

Denationalising state education will generate the need for new skills such as school bursars and a range of teaching opportunities for adults needing retraining from their redundant jobs. This could include using the abilities of those past normal retirement age and the resuscitation of trades in danger of being lost. Expect much experimentation as new means are introduced for meeting the needs of all generations.

Unwinding the health service will create a number of 'health boutiques' to cope with the need for a wide variety of sickness, ailments, injuries and probably also fads. This will need supervising by professionals but will attract a wide range of competent paramedics to fill a very varied demand.

Something similar will be needed for community-based welfare and security services as the current centralised organisations prove inadequate for dealing with an often fractured society. One could expect a revival of faith-based support groups as the need for greater standards are required. In addition, communities might also employ groups such as the Guardian Angels to patrol school grounds, buses, subways and streets – see earlier chapters.

There are at least two issues to be tackled to achieve this state: the first is how to train the increasing number of those who wish to become self-employed. The second is the creation of a Conservation and Security Agency (CSA) described earlier.

Even without the superstructure of regulations described earlier – or because of it – the failure-rate for small businesses is as high as 75% in the over three years from start-up. This can be very discouraging even for the most independent souls, but the odds can be much improved by copying an existing business though a franchising contract described earlier where the failure rate is around one-third that of unassisted start-ups.

Those countries in the West – and elsewhere – which have a healthy voluntary sector now have the opportunity not only to deal with unemployment but also the chance to create a new spirit of purpose, particularly among young people. This is in contrast to a rootless life, a drift into crime, the likelihood of rising racial tensions in difficult times and the prospect of swelling already crowded prisons.

What needs to be done to create new entrepreneurs

In summary, these are the items that need to be on the agenda of any new administration. This would apply not only to nations but in newly formed regions vying to attract new people as do the Swiss Cantons.

- Create an environment of low taxation, a stable currency and minimum interest rates.
- Expunge all regulations that would inhibit or discourage start-ups – even if this means abrogating international treaties. The others will see the wisdom of the action and most will follow suite.
- Create new tax-free zones around the major centres of research and excellence that will attract the best talents and good opportunities for financing.
- There should also be tax-advantaged zones around centres of trade and artistic excellence to attract vocational skills. Nations, particularly Germany and Switzerland, have developed a thriving small business sector that has largely provided the source of employment. The idea is for each nation to build on its own strengths and to offer these, and also sources of finance, elsewhere.
- Encourage venture capitalists to create new franchises from existing successful new businesses.
- Remove, if possible, the stigma of failure.
- Install a regime of encouraging bright émigrés.
- Encourage schools and society to create attractive venues.

Note: many new companies are born in recessions that will drive the new upswing when talents and assets are released from dying enterprises. This will be particularly true when public services and enterprises are denationalised.

Part 4.
Introduction to Managing Inflation and Deflation

Introduction

Debt is the greatest obstacle to recovery and there are four ways of overcoming it: repayment, taking a partial haircut, total default and inflation. History is replete with illustrations of them all, although only a few with repayment in full, such as Britain's settlement of First World War debts. Diocletian achieved debt reduction through inflation as did the French with the assignat and the Weimar Republic with the mark. The greatest destruction of debtors was during the Great Depression where debts nearly equivalent to the GDP in 1929 were wiped out in the United States over some ten years. There are also many instances of a haircut when all the major Latin American countries defaulted on their creditors during the 1930s – although there was a partial recovery after the war.

And what are we to make of the present? So far only Greece's creditors and Cypriot major depositors have been obliged to take a haircut, although there can be very few of the *cognoscenti* who actually believe that, in the midst of the greatest debt deflationary force in history, the huge wave will not overcome many nations and banks despite vast injections of liquidity. So far this manual has been concerned with describing these forces and suggesting policies that will mitigate the impact of the tsunami when it hits. Now this part suggests ways in which enterprises and nations can at least steer their entities through the turbulence.

Will it be debt destruction through inflation or deflation? The US experience of the 1930s suggests they will try to take the inflationary route, and the Germans the deflationary: the first primarily destroys creditors and the second both creditors and debtors. At a guess, politicians will go for the first as it will destroy their own debts while at the same time defrauding their fellow countrymen. There are two chapters to cover the most likely forces of debt destruction:

Chapter 1. Managing Inflation

Chapter 2. Managing Depressions

Part 4 Chapter 1.
Managing Inflation

Summary

The year 2000 ended the normal rhythm of booms and busts (known as the business cycle) where monetary means controlled an economy. Since then reducing interest rates will not create recovery, because we are now in a credit cycle. This is when excessive debt prevents monetary measures from working which is why very low interest rates and printing money on either side of the Atlantic have only attracted real estate and other bubbles. This condition is not understood by many governments which are employing progressively unwise measures to counter the downwave through 'initiatives' that only increase debt and deficits that only prolong the agony.

This has created considerable potential concerns for managers who may be unsure of the underlying economic conditions, the likely opportunities and downside risks that may arise. The purpose of this chapter is to set out what may be encountered during inflation, that is one means of destroying credit.

Introduction

Noble Laureate Milton Friedman held that inflation was always caused by monetary excess implying that it was under the control of the central bank. This worked in the early 1920s when the German Reichsbank printed money to such an extent that the hyperinflation forced the mark to devalue by over a trillion until the new *rentenmark* was issued. Nearer to the present, excessive money creation supply has created hyperinflation in several Latin American countries and in Zimbabwe.

When price rises are caused externally through an oil price increase, this would normally be deflationary – as individuals were obliged to spend less on discretionary purchases such as buying another car or planning a holiday. It only became inflationary – as it did by anyone who remembered the early 1970s – when the Fed effectively printed more money. The same effect would be through rapidly rising food prices or higher costs of imported goods or materials. The impact on a static economy is stagflation, considered later in the chapter.

We can also learn from what could become hyperinflation after central banks have created so much credit in an attempt to generate growth; then the currency falls dramatically and there is an uncontrollable rise in imported prices, as has happened several times in history. Hyperinflation has been used by politicians to eliminate their own debt and transfer wealth from individuals to the state. The result was the destruction of savings and pauperising all those on fixed incomes.

We know something of hyperinflation from the experience of Weimar Germany in the early 1920s, an event that is seared into German conscience. Then there were effectively three major phases which are worth exploring because we may be faced with the same phenomenon.

Phase 1

The rise in prices, and the reasons for it, are noticed by the cognoscenti who start taking appropriate management and investment decisions. However, the general public is hardly aware of the nature of inflation although shoppers become more price conscious, purchases are not delayed, wage demands remain subdued and banks may be persuaded to lend more. Price rises are still down the list of news items.

Phase 2

By now inflation is running in excess of 5% and is rising up the list of news items but governments, instead of monetary means, often try to introduce price and income controls, as they did in the early 1970s. These require that every time a firm takes action outside the guidelines they then have to be reported and monitored by bureaucrats who demand reasons. Of course there are many ways around such restrictions but this all takes up management time and effort.

However, soon there are demands for wage rises, strikes become endemic, the black market becomes rampant, barter become widespread, and pensioners and those on fixed incomes demand a rise in their emoluments. A constant feature in previous inflationary bouts is that politicians deliberately confuse the published statistics.

Phase 3

This stage is variously known as hyperinflation or the 'tipping point' when price rises exceed 25% a month, government bond issues can no longer be sold economically and the state can only survive by printing money; in the last stage of the German inflation in 1923, government revenues only paid for less than 0.1% of their expenditure.

Hyperinflation is generally the political chosen route to debt reduction for it eliminates their own liabilities and it effectively transfers wealth from individuals to the state. Companies with export earnings through foreign subsidiaries can generally squirrel away enough hard currency to conduct their affairs but this was not true in the final stages in Germany when, because of inflation, exports were no longer competitive.

For most of the population, who do not control the source of their income, life becomes progressively more difficult, with those of fixed incomes having to sell all their assets just to keep alive; the story is told by John Steinbeck on a visit to Germany. He was buying some apples when an old gentleman came up to admire his purchase but shaking his head because he could not afford them himself. The retail trade often ceased to function being outbid by the black market, so often people take the law into their own hands, raiding farms who refused to accept 'confetti currency' for their produce.

Eventually in November 1923 the chancellor Gustav Stresemann called in an independent banker Hjalmar Schacht who issued a new currency, the *rentenmark*, with a trillion of the old currency being exchanged for one rm. The Germans were fortunate, there was then the dollar to fix a rate; now paper currencies have been so debauched by central bankers that this time gold is likely to be the only anchor.

Management action during inflation

We can now identify appropriate management action at each phase of inflation.

Phase 1. The foothills.

This is how various sections might react.

<u>Customers</u>

Customers are obliged to spend more on food, energy and essentials that will rise in price as will most other products and services. As their income is unlikely to keep pace with prices they will be obliged to borrow more to fund their present standard of living or cut back. Those businesses unready for inflation will not put up their prices rapidly enough and will be in danger of failure through overtrading – see Part 4.

During inflation, companies should attempt to negotiate long-term supplier and short-term sales contracts that will minimise the cost of their purchases and give them maximum sales leverage. This will be particularly significant for strategic materials and services that could become very scarce and their price move up rapidly.

This is the time when unwise companies could try to buy their suppliers as their accountants tell them they can make two sets of profits. They may also be tempted to buy their customers, if they sell through distributors, to incorporate that profit as well. These actions, though possibly profitable in the short run, may prove disastrous when central banks are obliged to raise interest rates to quell inflation – as has happened many times in the past.

Undoubtedly the best policy, when inflation is still rampant, is to unwind any direct vertical ownership links when the prices become exponential, reduce inventory and shorten borrowings before the authorities raise interest rates. All these actions strengthen the balance sheet before the inevitable ensuing recession. They also provide the greatest flexibility when buying sound assets cheaply at the trough of the next downturn.

All classes of employees will demand a higher remuneration that should be granted providing the higher prices can be passed on to customers. In view of the caveat suggested in the previous paragraph, it might be wise to include a profit performance as part of the package which would aid individuals during inflation but keep costs down during the subsequent deflation.

If inflation is confined to one country there will be advantages in export selling to take advantage of a falling currency. However, taxes will still be levied so that it might be wise to sell, and take profits, through a subsidiary that will accumulate cash in a harder currency. The parent can then benefit from making purchases from abroad and paying their home taxes. Likewise, it would be wise to consider currency hedges on domestic funds.

Suppliers

Suppliers will face the mirror image of customers; they will attempt to negotiate long-term buying contracts and short-term sales deals. This is a period when keeping market share is important with standard products although, as the inflationary spiral reaches its climax, wise suppliers will prepare for the inevitable downturn; then inventories will be kept tight, competition will intensify, innovation helps to keep customers and hold margins and markets increasingly through the net.

At this point the market will start to differentiate:

- There will always be an opportunity at the top end of any market where quality and performance commands a premium price.
- As incomes become squeezed, most customers will seek the best deals at the functional end of the market.

Governments and central bankers

Those whose policies have brought on inflation will face a dilemma on how to stop it and remain in power because whatever they do will be unpopular. This then presents a major problem because most politicians are economically illiterate and have little sense of history so they are often at the mercy of bureaucratically-minded theorists. Also many will welcome inflation because it devalues debts.

If history is to repeat itself then politicians will institute the prices and income controls tried by the Nixon and Heath administrations in the early 1970s. A variation of these have been tried since Roman times, including rationing; they only encourage fraud and the black market.

A wiser approach would be raise interest rates slowly and let the market make the necessary adjustments while looking after the most vulnerable in society – see Part 3. At the same time governments should reduce their own spending for inflation makes it more difficult to collect taxes and raise bond issues with large budget deficits.

Phase 2

This is often the start of disintegration when the costs of most items, particularly imports, rocket as the currency falls rapidly. This is accompanied by serious labour unrest as unions attempt to help their members maintain their standard of living and unemployment starts rising. Those on fixed incomes such as pensioners will face disaster and politicians will be obliged to listen to this increasingly important voting group. By now, three groups of people will become more important and will probably be able to maintain their standard of living:

- With the increasing cost of providing oil-based supplies, those working in energy should do well.
- The same is true of those in food production, processing and distribution.
- There will always be a demand for precious metals as inflation increases.

As many young Germans discovered in the early 1920s, an academic qualification in art subjects was not in demand and many became apprentices in the areas above. There was always a demand for engineering graduates.

Retailers and suppliers

Retailers and suppliers will face similar problems to Phase 1 but the pressures will be greater as many suppliers will attempt to sell directly to customers so cutting out the retail margins. Retailers are likely to become progressively more specialised, and differentiated, offering services targeted at specific market sectors; service will be a premium. Pricing will continue to be a problem to keep up with the declining value of money. One approach in Germany was to cost an item in gold then continually adjust the price at the time of settlement. Another variant is for banks to offer a gold account where offers and settlements are priced in terms of the metal; this has the added advantage of maintaining the value of the account; other alternatives are to keep an account denominated in a firm currency such as the Swiss franc.

Governments

Governments which have not reduced their own spending will suffer rising deficits and find it increasingly difficult to collect taxes and sell debt. This has encouraged many politicians to attempt more regulation, prevent the use of other currencies and close tax loopholes – even to make their evasion a custodial crime; in France during the revolution a dozen men took a one-way trip to the guillotine! All this will be in vain as individuals will move much more quickly than the state, and inflation reaches its final phase.

Phase 3

This is the shortest and most violent when institutions start to fall apart, farmers and producers refuse to accept worthless notes, employees get paid twice a day, the velocity of money rockets and there is increasing civil disruption. There is also widespread despair; in Germany there were calls for the return of the Kaiser and Hitler chose this moment to mount the Bierkeller insurrection in November 1923.

Trade now disintegrates: the top end of the market remains reasonably normal while at the lower end has to adjust as the black market becomes widespread and there is total despair. Many made destitute descend to what the American psychologist Abraham Maslow defined as the lowest level – survival. Civil disobedience is widespread and the military is called in to keep order. In Germany the central government no longer commanded respect and the individual länder became more powerful, passing its own laws and issuing its own currency, as did many companies who opened shops for their employees who were paid twice a day.

This is the time for wise managements to prepare for the inevitable reaction when steps are taken to halt inflation and prepare for the inevitable depression, described in the next chapter. This means the reverse of managing inflation such as unwinding vertical subsidiaries, tightening cash flow, anticipating a rapid drop of volume, concentrating on the most significant accounts, strengthening the balance sheet and so on.

Having destroyed so many lives, the best service governments can do is to appoint a strong money-man to take charge, stop printing money and discounting bills, then take steps to help people back into some sort of equilibrium. In Germany, Prime Minister Gustav Stresemann appointed Hjalmar Schacht who created the *rentenmark*, with equivalence to the US dollar. However, now there is a major problem because nearly all the major fiat currencies will be suspect – so some form of gold standard will be necessary. In addition governments can take a number of remedial measures, not necessarily in order:

- Encourage the movement of food, particularly, into shops; this will not be easy because starving people tend to be violent.
- Restore a living income to pensioners.
- Clean up the many pseudo currencies that have been issued.
- Arrange haircuts to foreign holders of currency that have been defrauded by the devaluation.
- Reestablish credit – in Germany this was at some 20% of previous value which incensed those whose debts has been destroyed but this is essential to recommence trade.
- Give a credit to the government which will have been obliged to reduce its own expenditure to one third to avoid issuing bonds. It will not be possible to sell any term debt to external investors and only to domestic buyers under duress.
- Generate a make-work programme – see Part 3.
- Remove all restrictions to business start-ups except the laws of the land – see Part 3.
- Institute centres of excellence – see Part 3.
- Restore a devolved balance between the centre and the provinces.

Stagflation

This is the most dangerous condition of the three where manufacturing and service business is flat while at the same time input prices are being forced up as explained in Part 1. It is known as stagflation – as those who ran companies early in the 1970s will recognise with a degree of anguish. The government then tried to quell it through imposing strict conditions on prices and incomes and, although not the correct remedy, politicians might try it again. But how have we reached this state and what should we do about it?

To understand something of what we may be facing, let us take a brief look at 1970s. Then there was a rapid rise in financial speculation very similar to events leading up to the dot.com debacle in 2000, the 2007 rise in house prices and the Fed-inspired stock market blow off. The stagflation then was caused by war in the Middle East forcing up oil prices and similar conditions could arise again only this time relating to Iran. This is a brief summary: the war that ended in the Paris Peace accord of 1973 had released a great deal of additional spending in the US that was inflationary. Worried foreigners were removing gold and by August 1971 President Nixon decoupled the dollar from the gold standard; as the dollar declined, prices rose. In those days unemployment was considered a worse evil than inflation and the Fed did little to raise interest rates. Prices were already rising when OPEC increased the price of crude by ten times in 1973.

The Organisation of Petroleum Exporting Countries (OPEC) was started in the 1960s to stabilise the price of oil and protect the economies of the participating nations. The Arab nations of the organisation made OPEC political when in 1967 the Americans supported Israel in the six-days war; this later became overt in the 1973 Yom Kippur War when the price of crude was ratcheted upwards. Not knowing how to respond, the West allowed inflation to rocket. One of the reasons given by OPEC for increasing the oil price was the rising cost of food.

Climatic shifts have been the source of poor crops and high food prices over the centuries and the early 1970s were no exception. As the poor weather lowered crop yields, prices rose and the OPEC countries – many of them large importers – found their oil money bought less.

Now in 2015 there is the prospect of food price rises in some areas such as China; this will also apply to energy should conflicts break out in the Middle East. As inflation rises, so does speculation in financial assets and various forms of financial engineering – but be warned. In the subsequent recession these investments could prove disastrous.

This is a summary of how customers, suppliers and the government are likely to respond to this most unusual and dangerous condition.

Customers

Customers will be put in a dilemma: how to use their money. In the first place they will have to spend more on food, energy and essentials that could rocket in price. At the same time the cost of manufactured goods could fall making it cheaper to buy cars, washing machines and the like. As the government still tries to avoid recession by keeping interest rates low, this will mean that people will try to borrow more to keep up their standard of living but this too could become more difficult as credit becomes more tight; this places restrictions on buying more on credit. It will be all a matter of pricing power.

Those able to apply leverage to wage increases are likely to be those in food, energy and precious metals industries; those least able will be those in manufacturing, house building, those on fixed incomes and credit restricted services. Initially, those in public services will have some muscle but this will diminish as attempts to increase taxation will generate revolts. Those still with pricing power and with adequate savings are likely to be the only ones able to afford extras such as eating out, taking holidays or commissioning home extensions. Even those with inflation-proof pensions will be obliged to pull in their belts because the index is unlikely to track events.

At the same time business customers will try to negotiate purchase contracts of the longest possible duration at a fixed price so they can keep their costs down and benefit from any rising prices charged to their customers. Those with cash will attempt to quickly corner the market for material or service supplies likely to run short. This will be a roller coaster ride for everyone involved – just as it was in the early 1970s.

Suppliers

Suppliers will face the mirror image of customers. They will find rising competition selling to growth businesses requiring considerable innovation to meet tightening standards. Selling to manufacturers or to cash-strapped end-users will need simpler and cheaper products to keep the business; the ability for these accounts to pay will become increasingly strained as bankruptcies soar.

On no account should suppliers attempt to retain market share on reduced margins as those who try will be squeezed and costs will rise. Wise suppliers will attempt to find niches in a much more segregated market place where diversification prevails. Those supplying essential materials or services should avoid negotiating long-term contracts at fixed prices. Selling directly to the end user will become commonplace.

The clamour to end stagflation will be re-enforced by older people on pensions and those on fixed incomes who have increased their voting power, but who have seen their income falling behind prices and their standard of living collapse. All these lead to demands on the authorities to control rising prices by raising interest rates, an act that will be inevitably lead to a deep recession, even a depression.

Governments and central bankers

Governments and central bankers are faced with a dilemma. If they try to control deflation by keeping down interest rates they only increase inflation; conversely raising rates to quell inflation only adds another deflationary turn of the screw. Usually central bankers initially will not try to end inflationary trends too severely but will be inevitably obliged to raise interest rates as rising prices get out of hand.

As with inflation, left-leaning governments are likely to introduce price and income controls but with stagflation this is only likely to be needed on the sectors of the economy associated with pricing power such as energy and most commodities. This action will only generate a black market that will hit those on fixed incomes the hardest.

The most sensitive approach would be to raise interest rates to just above inflation and to encourage those on fixed incomes, where possible, to find part-time jobs. Some imaginative programmes for this are set out elsewhere. Others would be to set up local barter schemes whereby individuals could offer a range of services in exchange for credits available to buy food and other essentials. It is at these times that individuals tend to be at their most creative in an attempt to stave off what could become civil unrest and economic chaos.

Part 4 Chapter 2.
Managing Depressions

Summary

This is a phenomenon that business people have been obliged to discover in the first decades of the new century when debts are so large that monetary measures no longer stimulate the economy: it's what the great American economist Irving Fisher described as debt/deflation. It is also called the credit cycle and although central banks may print money, it has little impact on reviving the economy while the velocity of money and the money supply remains subdued.

In the 1930s it took ten years in the US for excessive debt to be wrung out of the system. Now the total debt build-up, related to GDP, is approaching double that of 1929, so despite short periods of apparent recovery, it would be prudent for managers to plan for a long haul. This chapter consists of what history shows are the ways of managing during deflation.

However, as the earlier chapter showed, it will not be a matter of managing another 1930s debt destruction by default, for this time debt could be destroyed by hyperinflation/hyperstagflation or collapsing currencies – even repayment! Unfortunately this will leave an even more tragic legacy than eighty years ago with many prices, especially food, water and energy probably remaining at a high level.

About depressions

It is greatly unfortunate that the abiding memory for the United States is the fear of another Great Depression for, on reflection, this was a period of very considerable innovation. This was also true in Britain, and in both countries this drove not only the later tremendous war effort but also created the technologies that generated the subsequent recovery. This is not true of inflation-driven periods of debt destruction as we learned in the previous chapter. Consider the periods of boom and bust described in Part 1, for during depressions there were always technologies that drove the subsequent recovery, such as these experienced in the first three completed cycles.

- *Before the start of the first wave from 1790* there was the sulphuric acid process, quinine, the steam locomotive, puddling furnaces, the first Atlantic steamship crossing, electric telegraphs, the rotary press, anaesthetics, the screw lathe, the cotton gin with replaceable parts, sewing machines and so on.
- *Before the start of the second wave in the 1850s* amongst others there was the invention of the internal combustion engine, oil drilling, dynamite, electric railways, transformers, bicycles, the steam turbine, combine harvesters, the Atlantic telegraph and the like.
- *Before the start of the third wave in the 1890s* there was the mechanical record player, portable cameras, motion pictures, motor cycles, monotype, x-rays, the diesel engine, electric automobiles, oxy-acetylene welding, viscose rayon, electric washing machines, synthetic rubber, mass production, amongst others.
- *Among other inventions that drove the fourth wave that occurred during the 1930s* included Freon refrigeration, gas turbines, PVC, electron microscopes, nylon, catalytic cracking, helicopters, jet engines, penicillin, ball-point pens, phototype, cortisone, Polaroid cameras, xerography, oxygen steel-making, diesel locomotives and others.

The inventions likely to drive the next wave are set out in Part 5.

Managing depressions

Those managing businesses since 2000 and in previous decades have had the experience of a deflationary environment even though this has not penetrated many political circles. While during inflation there is a concentration on the operating statement and standard products, with deflation this is quite the opposite. The great economist Joseph Schumpeter argued that any manager can profit when demand exceeds supply, but it takes brains to manage when the position is reversed!

The most critical decision a manager can make is to strengthen the balance sheet and take steps to reduce the break-even point. The next most important decision is to put resources into innovation. However, there are tactical decisions to be made in managing a business during extreme deflation.

This is how people may expect to react to managing a business in these conditions.

Customers

Customers should be seeking to maximise their cash flow even at the expense of margins which is why a cash-rich supplier will be able to get a better price in exchange for good settlement terms. At the same time consumers will be seeking to negotiate long-term sales and short-term supply contracts. Most importantly, all marketing effort will be to secure and retain customers through special offers, improved service, innovation and so on. They will be reminded of Alfred Sloan's advice in *My Years With General Motors*, "Every lost customer was a tragedy and new accounts hard to find."

Suppliers

Suppliers will be facing a mirror image as customers but here the emphasis will be on innovation and maintaining excellent support packages to retain accounts against increasingly fierce competition. As the squeeze on margins continues, customers often delay purchases to negotiate a lower price but may be encouraged by an added feature or better performance, not to wait. For example during the 1930s, the advent of chilled food encouraged the purchase of refrigerators for many households despite tight cash flows.

Another feature to be considered is the advent of direct selling by suppliers such as farmers directly to the public – as they did in Japan during the 1990s. Although in this cycle farm prices will remain firm, the principle may well be applied across a range of merchandise when one could find co-operatives formed to sell extensive products directly to the public and through the net; then, if these need servicing, individual engineers would be appointed to support the product. Any move such as this could force retailers to specialise in a particular product or service.

The most critical policy decision is innovation which is the subject of Part 5.

Governments

Governments may feel that the way to move out of a recession is to step up public spending, even if this means raising taxes and greatly increase borrowing. This policy is almost certainly folly as is evident by so many politicians in 2015 being reluctant to make the important decisions to bring their economies and peoples into an equilibrium as explained in Part 3. The Roosevelt administration attempted this method in 1933, France in 1936 and latterly Japan in the 1990s. Now the US and other nations are attempting to disprove history despite crowding out the private sector and raise debt still further.

In 1941 Henry Morganthau, Roosevelt's treasury secretary, commented that the government had spent a great deal of money during the depression and had achieved very little. By contrast Britain in the 1930s reduced government spending, lowered taxes and eliminated most regulations to encourage entrepreneurs. This policy succeeded in creating many new industries, generating employment and raising prosperity – almost alone among the developed nations.

Part 5.
Technologies Driving
the Digital Age

The driving force of any new wave are the technologies developed during periods of distress. This is an understandable conclusion, for the need to innovate during these times is essential if suppliers are to command the attention of buyers and to provide the motive power for the next upswing. Up to the present, innovations have tended to be concentrated on using the power of nature to make life easier and, in earlier periods, were often driven by empiricism. Now the developments are likely to focus on the essentials of matter in order to understand and harness the power of the atom in its several forms. These are just some of the technologies, apart from the communication revolution, likely to drive the Digital Age and are already starting to bring manufacturing back into developed countries.

Water conservation and use is a priority in countries such as Israel, the eastern Mediterranean and elsewhere that have suffered from water shortages over centuries. However, as aquifers run dry and ground water is pumped out, these measures will need to become more widespread. Here much of the technology is empiric such as avoiding evaporation where possible, concentration on supplying water where it is needed, conserving run-offs and so on. There is also likely to be the need for more localised water treatment plants to reduce, as far as possible, wasteful leakage. The section under biotechnology suggests there will also be increased emphasis on adapting cultivars to more stressful conditions such as lower rainfall and brackish water.

Hydroponics and Vertical Farming are subsets of hydroculture where plants are grown in soilless conditions and nutrients are supplied directly to the roots in a carbon dioxide rich atmosphere. Conditions can be static or continuous where root sprays are provided automatically to generate optimum growth. While these techniques are well understood and implemented, there are variations such as vertical farming where the plants are circulated under ideal conditions of heat, light and nutrients and the time for harvesting is sensed automatically. Both these techniques have the advantages of reducing waste to market, working under adverse weather conditions, being relatively free of pests, conserving water and so on. They do suffer from being reliant on continuous power and are expensive to set up compared with food grown naturally. The same principles of monitoring and directing are being applied to other aspects of farming such as to dairy herds.

Material technologies have been largely based on the alloying, melting, casting, forming and machining of metals and new composites, and it was these techniques that drove the industrial era. Metals are important for specialist applications of working under temperature and pressure but where tensile strength and lightness are needed, techniques such as carbon fibres and nanocellulose are becoming significant. A filament thread is made up of thousands of grains – which are tubes a few micrometers in width and made up into sheets with a regular pattern. The basic properties of strength or firmness depend upon the orientation of the grains and in manufacture, carbon fibre cloth is impregnated with epoxy resin layer by layer in an automatic process; when cured it has the strength of steel but is much lighter. It is already being used to make a one-piece chassis for cars where light weight is important, also for main wing spars. There is a variant of carbon called graphine which, at a single atom depth, is stronger than the equivalent steel sheet and has excellent electrical qualities.

New developments suggest that materials can now be adapted to change shape in response to electric currents; one application is to elongate the trailing edge of an aircraft's wing to form a flap when landing. Now whole wings are being made of composites which never corrode. Another use of 'smart' materials is to generate a current when exposed to water and wind; at present this can only generate small impulses but researchers believe this could have much wider applications. There are also developments in a military sense for materials to change colour to match different environments, and to be ballistics-resilient.

Biotechnology is the technique of adapting live organisms mainly for medical and for human purposes. These ideas are not new, having developed from when mankind first observed, then selected and domesticated, the most edible plants and creatures. However, during the First World War Chaim Weizmann developed a process for making acetone from starch then during the 1920s experimenters such as Henry Wallace in the US selectively bred cultivars such as corn to suit varying soil and climatic conditions. Since then these are some of the branches that have been developed:

- There is a study in pharmacology for adapting medicines and other antidotes to the individual having analysed the genetic structures they were designed to cure.

- Processes now also target individual complaints such as hepatitis, cancers, arthritis and other diseases often by identifying the errant cell, isolating it, and preventing it from spreading.

- Genetic targeting allows analysts to identify a harmful gene then, through growing a curative cell, splice this into a patient's DNA. It is argued that new organs such as teeth can be re-grown using these techniques – not unlike alligators.

- As suggested earlier, crop genetics can be modified to give the plant immunity to some pests and insecticides. In Israel olives have been adapted to thrive in brackish water found in an aquifer; it is reported that these trees yield a greater crop than many grown naturally.

- It is hoped that organisms can be adapted to reduce an ore to its natural element.
- Although not strictly biotechnological, it is thought that mental processes can be stimulated by energising specific parts of the brain.

Geoengineering is an attempt to counter concerns that the earth is warming through the release of human-generated carbon dioxide. Various ideas are being explored, among them are sprinkling iron on the oceans to stimulate plankton that consume CO2, and on land the large-scale planting of trees would have the same effect. Efforts are being made to capture CO2 from large emitters and thought is being given to methods of reflecting sunlight.

Additive manufacturing or 3D printing is a proven method of manufacturing an object directly from a computer-aided design. One process works by injecting plastic or metal particles in suspension through a stylus, similar to inkjet-printing, onto a plate. As the laminar image is formed from the CAD shape, it is then cured and the bath lowered fractionally for the next layer to be formed. Moving parts can be installed at the same time and the technique offers innovators the opportunity to print one-offs which can then be test marketed before attempting to invest in a production process. These techniques will be integrated into many more 'smart' factories where minimum order quantities can be rapidly executed to meet the demands of fast-changing markets and bringing manufacturing back to the West.

Nanotechnology is a very new science dealing with particles the width of four of the smallest known units, a hydrogen atom, or a billionth of a metre. The technology was first popularised by Eric Drexler, who saw the potential for making assemblies molecule-by-molecule long before the science could catch up with his ideas. These concepts go one stage further than 3D Printing by directing individual molecules into their required shape; in this way, it is argued that many different metals or plastics could be formed in a continuous process into an assembled product. Ultimately anything, including food, could be created in this way but currently such items as nanotubes are being used in desalination processes or as film applied as a waterproof coating.

Robotics have been a dream ever since Leonardo da Vinci but since the war they have been increasingly used in industrial process to automate repetitive functions such as in auto manufacture or in assembly. These remotely controlled machines are powered electrically, hydraulically or pneumatically depending upon their size to move arms and hand equivalents to grasp, move and present items for the next process, and by their nature can be programmed; they can also use sensors to give a more precise movement. Apart from automation, robots are widely used by the military to inspect suspected explosive devices and they are being brought into the field for surveillance and, if needed, into action such as unmanned aeronautical vehicles to scan and then attack targets. There are great hopes to produce robots to help with the housework, and experiments are far advanced to automate driving a car with associated sensors.

Conventional energy development has become more critical with the shortage of new, easily accessible, oil fields, the increasing expense of exploration and military action curtailing supplies. Recently, the new technology centres in Britain are a source of new ideas. Although nuclear power is under suspicion from the recent Japanese disaster it is still a potent source of electrical energy and there is the future promise of molten salt technology. This operates at atmospheric pressure, is 30 times more efficient as a nuclear fuel and shuts down automatically in the event of an accident; proponents argue that it can generate electricity competitive with gas at 5.5p per KWh. Further ahead there is the option of cold fusion, the energy released from uniting two atoms of deuterium safely. For oil production there is the well-tried Fischer Tropsch process of extracting oil from coal and there may be increasing opportunities for using hydrogen in conjunction with fuel cells. Shale gas is being increasingly used in the US and elsewhere to make nations more independent of imported energy.

Part 6.
One Man's Understanding
of the Digital Age

This manual has been primarily concerned with how history helps us to navigate through the appalling legacy of the Industrial era that started nearly 300 years ago when it released the powerful creative forces that drove unprecedented economic growth. Unfortunately this also encouraged the centralisation of political, financial and military power that enabled ambitious politicians to wage increasingly deadly wars and, in an attempt to stay in power, bribed votes by assisting a rising number of people to rely on the state. Even in the US and UK around half the population is dependent upon handouts from the state which left-leaning politicians are most reluctant to curtail. Although it was not realised at the time, the events of 2008 should have been the trigger for wiser heads to prevail but sadly this was not the case and the spending and borrowing continued.

However we have to clear away the previous detritus before we can expect a sound recovery; now we have to try to identify some of the features I believe will form part of the new landscape.

In the first place the vast majority of the population will have to adjust to a lower standard of living following the collapse of debt, an event that is critical before the new era could begin; all the talk of potential recovery was a cruel deception by politicians who claimed to have beaten the business cycle and hoped we would be able to carry on managing as before. We have been here before during wartime when, although almost everyone had to take a haircut, only the infirm had not got a job. Something similar should happen now because, as previous parts have suggested, there would be a calamitous loss of confidence.

This is because the day of large governments and the welfare state are over as they are unaffordable and any continuation of the illusion would result in the much more efficient private sector being increasingly squeezed. The cult of smaller activity will almost certainly be true of corporations and institutions, except in exceptional cases where huge resources are needed such as in energy prospecting or new research into techniques such as cold fusion. When, or if, the cost of oil rises in excess of $200/barrel, the government, social and business climate will be one of extreme deflation forcing a rapid decentralisation when the previous structure becomes no longer affordable. Apart from those having a direct input to an activity, all those in staff functions will live remotely but be connected electronically in some form or another to avoid costly travel.

This diaspora will have powerful social consequences of reviving previously run-down rural areas being settled with people having energy and initiatives. Activities such as security, refuse collection, schools, healthcare, welfare, churches, local amenities, libraries, local justice and so on will be organised, funded and managed locally with the diminution of the need for local authorities; professional services such as policing will be concerned with crime solving and technologies will link them to local communities where groups such as the Guardian Angels will keep the peace. This will lead to a wide variety of different political systems ranging from the laissez faire to forms of Marxism. Perhaps the development of the Israeli kibbutzim will provide some models. However, each one will need to provide an attractive environment to attract entrepreneurs.

The regeneration is likely to apply to most cities made up by amalgamating nearby towns and villages. Many of these retain some form of their original character and could revert, orientated as they were before, around a particular skill or resource. These new groupings could create a greater feeling of belonging that is often so absent within a conurbation developing their own sense and feeling that is often still found in many towns.

These new groupings will not suit everybody, neither will working from home, so part of the work of the new communities will be to create new business centres. These initially will use existing buildings such as a pub, village hall or a church part-time as a centre where individuals can work, use the latest communication technology, arrange meetings, entertain and conduct their business. This is likely to become the hub of managing the local unit where those offering a range of services can seek business including the self-employed.

The huge retraining programme described in Part 3 that is necessary both to help the unemployed, and those made redundant from the demise of old industries, will help create a number of individuals with different skills. These will be needed both to support the new corporations that are bound to be started locally, but also individual households with a range of services. Where money is tight, use of a local bartering system such as LETS (Part 3) would not only bring liquidity to the community but also put people in touch with the available services. Other activities would change too.

A form of politics, probably on the Swiss model (Part 3) will be essential if the state is to take a smaller role having unwound health, education and welfare to locally run services. However there will need to be some national direction of matters such as possible human or animal epidemics, national transport and the like. High transport costs will necessarily demand that many staff functions are devolved allowing many buildings to be converted into dwellings or remote business centres, as mentioned earlier. National politicians will probably become part-time and only meet for two monthly periods at a time, three times a year. The same will be true of part-time politicians in local authorities although, once again, most of their work will have been much devolved and only a core need remain.

Although many could resent this, probably up to one half of the population will be working for themselves or in small groups supplying services to larger units. However, the Conservation and

Security Agency (CSA) and National Recovery Agency (NRA) (Part 3) will still be needed as it will take a while to wean people off the incubus of the welfare state that paid people to do nothing. It is also needed for disaster relief and as a pre-training element for some form of National Guard or Territorial Army that would probably be managed at the state or county level. We can also expect centres of excellence offering apprenticeships for those unable to benefit from a university training. But business will be responsible for the recovery.

Technology will be the driving force of any new era with engineers being more in demand than accountants or lawyers. During the 1930s in Britain there was the political and economic environment that encouraged entrepreneurs to experiment and meet the rising demand for transportation, radios, domestic appliances, aircraft and the like; however, these were all businesses needing an increasing labour force. Now the new industries will reflect technologies such as bio- and nanotechnology, new forms of energy creation, new materials, communications and robotics, to grow in the harsher conditions described in Part 1. Most of these will need fewer but more specialised people supported by the individual or collective groupings described earlier.

With the end of fiat currencies and a return to some form of gold standard (Part 3), funding for many activities is likely to be more local as many of the big financial institutions will have been wiped out in the expected wild stagflationary, and then deflationary, environment. Instead, as happened two hundred years ago, the banks will be more local in character started by wealthy entrepreneurs and business people. With the new communications, some would become national to deal with international business.

Unwinding the previous industrial era and the welfare state amidst the baleful influence of the tsunamis will demand the finest managerial and political brains that any country can mobilise, on the scale of wartime, that will demand a huge constructive effort by all; of particular importance will be the rescue of millions of children growing up in homes where no one has ever known work. Those making the effort will be rewarded by a new era when each individual has a value that can make a contribution and may be fulfilled physically and emotionally – if not spiritually.

Afterword

There have been many discontinuities in history with some major ones occurring every five hundred years or so. This book has concentrated on the parallels with the last half millennium, for this period was rich in great events that have convergence with the present, and help us put this into perspective so we can observe more closely how people behaved. However, history never quite repeats itself and earlier chapters have identified the changes, their nature and the speed with which they may explode.

It is doubtful how many of those living around the year 1500 knew the implication of the events that were unfolding, but having written the previous chapters, it is beholden upon me to identify where the changes may be expected and how groups of people may be forewarned by far-seeing people. I have done this in three areas: business, the individual and nationally in an attempt to identify the several strands and to see how these might unite and unfold.

This is how the chairman of a national business confederation might address its members.

Fellow delegates, I would like to give you some background to the work we have done with the government and from our own resources and our conclusions of what we believe lies ahead; you will hear separately the action our nation's chief executive intends to take, now we will actively consider how this impacts on our members.

The huge build-up of public and private debt over the last few years could never have been based on any ability to pay it back – in particular, the large number of speculative operations engaged in by financial institutions have nothing to do with the creative activities that are the essence of most business. As an aside, your council has agreed – despite strenuous opposition from our banking colleagues –

to recommend that investment should be separated from commercial banking, as concluded by the Vickers Committee, as a first step in protecting the banking system, as I shall explain later.

I have always worked on the principle that whenever there has been an exponential rise of any activity, such as the 2007 property debacle or the very rapid increase in public and private debt on both sides of the Atlantic, there will be a subsequent and very rapid fall as there was in the US from 1930 to 1932; the diagram is in the pack assembled for each delegate (see Part 1). This decline often takes away at least half of the earlier rise taking with it all those unwise enough not to have read the signals.

Consequently I fear we face a roller coaster of climatic and economic change that will test to the utmost the ability of each of us to plan ahead, to read the multi-faceted signs and to manage the transition. First I would like to identify what is in store for us, the areas most likely to succeed, then the various support operations that we are planning.

There are several ways in which credit can be reduced. The most obvious is that it can be paid back – a most unlikely event now. The debtor could default, as many Latin American countries did in the 1930s with the creditors receiving at best 30 cents to the dollar years later; this is clearly the reason why the Eurozone is having so much difficulty in establishing its rescue operations. There is the possibility of a structured repayment deal, but the most likely outcome is the destruction of debt through several causes such as currency destruction, inflation or deflation.

The size of any write-down is staggering and is likely to be in excess of $30 trillion or twice the US GDP; there would be an equivalent fall on the eastern seaboard of the Atlantic. Any collapse of this scale would wipe out the capital of most creditors, which is why we have advocated the modern equivalent of the Glass-Steagall Act passed in 1933 early in the Roosevelt administration. However, credit is not the only pressure for, as I suggested earlier, there are powerful supply-side limits on food supplies which could make the time ahead one not of hyperinflation, but hyperstagflation; this is when many commodity prices rise rapidly against a backdrop of a declining economy. You would now wish me to identify some of those business areas that we in the council believe would be likely to thrive in these circumstances.

Food production, processing, retailing and distribution will remain a growth area for at least ten years due to supply-side restrictions and the time it will take to introduce remedial measures.

Although in the doldrums now, energy in various forms could be much in demand as alternatives are found to make nations more self-reliant. To this end I suspect many of the environmental concern to fuels such as coal will be swept aside.

There will be a demand for items of intrinsic and lasting value that defy turbulent currency and other markets.

We believe that circumstances will oblige politicians to unwind many of the activities that comprise the welfare state. This will provide opportunities for many entrepreneurs to offer equivalent services more efficiently and effectively than before.

We can expect governments and companies to shed many activities, which is why we expect a powerful growth of people moving to rural areas to supply devolved services including banking.

It follows that there will be many more self-employed people who will demand devices and systems to help them be more independent and efficient.

Unlike the past fifty years of relative stability, we anticipate the acceleration of entrepreneurs forming groups to perfect a particular product or service, then selling these, before starting another activity.

Finally I would like to describe the sort of services we are planning to offer our members in an effort to both inform and support those unused to turbulent markets.

We will be assembling a team of experienced business people in different disciplines to provide regular reports of events and their implications. Some time ago information was scarce, now it is abundant so we are planning to generate an understanding and knowledge of events to assist our members in constructing agendas and helping them to make business decisions.

Next we plan a fee-based service for individual corporations whereby the critical factors, be they the cost of commodities, interest rates or currency variations and so on, be monitored and reported on from what might be termed 'a shadow board'.

We recognise that many of the situations I have outlined may be strange to many chief executives so we are planning to offer a simulator whereby the board's reaction and decisions to different set of economic inputs may be modelled and the results discussed. In this way we hope that, coupled with the measures set out earlier, we may help companies be at or ahead of the curve.

We are always open to comments on what we propose and how we may be of better service to our members. God speed and I wish you every success.

This is how a father might write to a newly graduated economist.

Very dear son,

Now you are leaving university, you will be contemplating the next step and will have written to many prospective employers. I do not want to discourage you but there are a lot of graduates with good degrees on the same path so I don't want you to become too unhappy if they do not leap for you. Being turned down for a good job is very disappointing and after a bit one gets the feeling that everything you have done and all the hard work you have put in is wasted. But do not be too upset, just try another tack.

We are living in very turbulent times when the unexpected becomes the norm and a seemingly secure job can become obsolete by some market fluctuation. As you are aware, your elder sister, with a degree in computer science, is doing a part-time nursing course and I think you should be doing something of the same. You have always been very practical so why not consider a course in plumbing, decorating, carpentry or whatever trade suits your fancy; all these skills will continue to be in demand – as will being a waiter. Always remember to keep in touch with your friends and contacts; it will be the age of networking where groups of people will get together for a project to find some space in the market then, in all probability, move on. Our American cousins call this 'catching the fast buck'.

You will ask me what I would do if something happened to my accountancy firm – which is something that has given me much thought – as has a steep fall in the value of my pension fund. I believe there will be many smaller firms starting up so with a few friends I am planning to start a one-stop professional firm giving accountancy, legal, property and other professional advice; we will not be charging the fees we used to but there should be a steady income.

Finally I must tell you what your grandfather is planning for his home town. When they threatened to shut the library and remove the policemen, he arranged a meeting, in conjunction with the local council, in the hall. The idea is to make the library into a community centre run by volunteers under a paid manager and to create their own watchdog to keep an eye on the town. He has heard of a group called the Guardian Angels and will be recruiting among the able of the town to be trained by these people. Finally he is proposing a local bartering system to provide a range of service, ranging from babysitting to language tuition and help with filling in a tax form. Do spare some time to go and see what he is doing.

Your mother and I hope to see you soon,

Your loving father.

This is how a thoughtful leader might address their nation.

My fellow countrymen, I would like to tell you the results of a strategic review conducted by my colleagues and myself on the threats and opportunities we face in the next ten to fifteen years and the measures we will take both to safeguard our country and to be a loyal ally to our friends. We believe that the threats facing us are on a parallel with that of war and the measures we need to take are, in our opinion, fundamental. First the threats:

Despite the misgivings of some committed individuals, we have concluded that the natural climatic threats are infinitely greater than anything we as people can create. We have only to consider the recent flooding, droughts and earthquakes in many areas of the globe caused by seismic action, solar variations and oceanic temperature changes to attest to this truth. This decision has led to a number of other decisions that I will explain in due course.

Next, again against the misgivings of some academics, we have concluded that the primary threat to a recovery are the very high debt levels in most countries that misguided policies have only made more acute. Unfortunately, these policies have also made it increasingly likely that debt can only be expunged by high levels of inflation that threaten a very large number of people and lead most likely to reduced national output. These may become stagflationary when rapidly rising commodity prices impose on a static economy. I will come to some of the measures we propose.

Unfortunately, the climatic situation has made wars over water and food more likely. Following the reports from the Middle East, and the unrest in other parts of the world, the situation has obliged us to strengthen the armed forces. To this end we will be amalgamating the Royal Air Force with the Royal Navy and Army; this has not been an easy decision considering the wonderful service given to our country by the RAF, but we have had to work within a plan of financial stringency that obliges us to drastically curtail the expense of a separate service and the civilian content of military support.

Now we would invite all those from whatever persuasions to join us in what we must conclude is a mission of national necessity on the scale of wartime.

First we plan to reduce the government and state expenditure to one third of national output from lower than half at present. This is essential if we are to allow private enterprise to lead the recovery, for it is a mistake to believe that governments can perform this service. This will mean replacing state-backed services with those provided privately and locally through different methods of funding. We will be setting up a number of working parties to which those involved will be invited.

To safeguard the nation's food supplies, we will be encouraging farmers to bring every acre of arable land into production. Where there are shortfalls in national demand we will be encouraging the food industry to make forward purchases of the balance. We have already curtailed the use of crops for producing methanol.

We also recognise that disruption in the fuel-rich areas of the world is highly likely to raise the cost of crude oil to levels that would cripple the commercial life of our country. We have held discussions with the major oil companies who have agreed, as a matter of urgency, to set up coal cracking plants based on Sasol Pty's Fischer-Tropsch technology to produce fuel oil. We have abundant coal in the country and will be encouraging electricity producers to erect low-emission coal-burning electricity generators. We also recognise that other sources of energy, such as safer nuclear reactors, cold fusion, shale energy and hydrogen, will become more viable.

We are very aware of how any economic disruption will impact on people's lives and in particular the young who fail to find a job and the more elderly whose pensions have been destroyed by inflation. To this end we will be initiating a number of measures:

The first will be a work and training programme that will require all those who wish to receive state support to join. There will be several levels of opportunities: local, national and also international. The aim is to give work experience and training to all displaced by the Digital Age on the principle that all, except for the totally disabled, can make a useful contribution. This will also help to quell rising crime among young people whom society has apparently chosen to disregard. These activities would particularly attract the help of retired servicemen and others with a wide variety of skills.

Next there will be a national apprenticeship plan based on centres of trade excellence and vocational competence. There will be incentives for those taking on apprentices and help for those wishing to set up their own activities. We will remove every constraining legislation on entrepreneurship.

We plan that there will be opportunities for retired people to help in the training programme to pass on their skills and also help to provide services for those setting up on their own.

We have become increasingly aware of threats to our security from religious fundamentalists and will be preparing contingency plans to revoke human rights legislation and review introducing Defence of the Realm legislation should this be necessary.

These are all programmes that will involve other people; we will also be considering how best governments can function more efficiently at less cost as we are well aware how our productivity lags seriously behind the private sector. Our review will include closing ministries and dispersing many functions.

We foresee that little recovery can take place until debt has declined to reasonable levels, for any inflation is bound to be followed by a deep recession. However, this is also a cleansing process that has, always in the past, stimulated the new activities that will trigger the new upswing. In our opinion this will provide many opportunities for individual enterprise and a much more open society where all are valued for making a contribution.

I have recently read a passage from the Book of Revelation that might be appropriate to describe why I am optimistic about what lies ahead.

Then I saw a new heaven and a new earth; for the first heaven and the first earth had passed away, and the sea was no more... and God himself will be with them; and He will wipe away every tear from their eyes and death shall be no more, neither shall there be mourning nor crying nor pain any more, for the former things have passed away. And He who sat upon the throne said, 'Behold, I make all things new.'

Revelation, Chapter 21

Amen to that.

William Houston
St James'
June 2015

The follow-up books to Global Recovery Manual will be published by ADVFN Books in 2016:

The Digital Age Handbook: Empowering the Individual
2015 to 2025: Through the Dark Decade
Handbook for Reducing the Break-even Point

Index

About the Author

William Houston joined the Royal Navy at the end of the Second World War and specialised in weapons. After leaving the service, he qualified as a chartered engineer and an administrator before embarking on a career as a company recovery specialist either directing or advising a wide range of industrial and commercial concerns. For ten years he was an industrial advisor to a merchant bank before taking up a career in writing. His first book *Avoiding Adversity* was published in 1989 advising managers how to survive the following recession.

He then became interested in the cycles of the world including economics, climate, politics, warfare, disease, and wrote *Riding the Business Cycle*, *Future Storm* and *Water: the Final Resource* – the latter two co-authored with Robin Griffiths, a noted technical analyst and investor.

He subsequently became the principal of The School of Global Recovery.

Previous books:

Avoiding Adversity
Meltdown
Riding the Business Cycle
Future Storm
Water: the Final Resource by Houston & Griffiths (Harriman House 2008)
The Manual of Global Recovery
How the United States Recovered
How Britain Recovered
Two Recoveries and Two Re-Orientations
2015 – 2025 The Dark Decade
Handbook for Reducing the Break-even Point
The Digital Age, Empowering the Individual
School of Global Recovery

For further information visit www.globalrecoverycenter.org.

Reviews of
William Houston's Books

Daily Mail: "Houston's work is fascinating"

The Times: "The Chancellor of the Exchequer might well be advised to lay aside his Treasury briefing paper to read *Meltdown* – the book describes a chilling scenario of worldwide financial collapse, and also functions as a manual to take advantage of the ensuing opportunities."

Financial Times: "William Houston is prepared to be unorthodox and that is important when the green shoots of conventional economic wisdom have proved so misleading."

Lord Rees-Mogg: "I advise all those interested in the future to read *Riding the Business Cycle*."

Bill Meridian of Cycles Research: "*Water: The Final Resource* by William Houston and Robin Griffiths. This easily-readable book presents complex data about the earth and it's precious resource Water. The current trends point towards greater demand and flat to declining supply."

James Puplava, CEO of PFS Group and Host of the Financial Sense News Hour, San Diego, California: "...Two tsunamis, one financial/economic and the other climatic are about to converge and unleash their destructive force upon the world's economy... For investors, *Triple Tsunamis* is your compass to help navigate the troubled time ahead... One of the most thought provoking books I have recently read."

Stephen Hill, CEO of Anglo-Sino Capital Partners: "Bill Houston reflects a lifetime of close observation, induction and erudition. This work has practical lessons for everyone, from the President/Prime Minister down to each of the unemployed."

Spectator Business: "'Water is going to control the political, economic and social agenda over the next twenty years,' Houston says. 'It is going to be the major military issue for the next generation.'"

The Guardian on *Water: the Final Resource:* "...even so, their main topic is an important one – the politics of water usage as it planetary changes. They explain dams, irrigation, water recycling and desalination, and consider future impacts of water on crops and population."

Dr Marc Faber, editor of the *Gloom, Boom and Doom report*: "Mr Houston is right when he says that the economic problems are not 'the only difficulties' facing us. In *Triple Tsunamis* Mr. Houston shows that in future, water and food shortages are likely to bring about conflicts and how they might affect asset markets. Houston's analysis of the 'Immense Forces of Change' is fascinating."

Stephen Lewis, Chief Economist, Monument Securities: "William Houston challenges the prevailing wisdom that governments can lead a nation out of recession. In his latest book, *Triple Tsunamis*, policymakers have not yet begun to come to grips with the root cause of the financial breakdown, the unbridled expansion of debt at all levels of the economy over many years. They are also paying no attention to how changes in weather conditions are likely to affect what is arguably the most important economic question of all, how people are to feed themselves. He sets the challenges facing responsible decision-makers, whether they are running businesses from day to day or are charged, as leaders, with attempting to establish a policy that nurtures enterprise, in the context of the long-term cycles that clearly emerge from the historical record.

There is no reason for despair, Mr Houston maintains. The technological cycle has been one of the most important features of human development. There are striking parallels between the present-day revolution in communications technology and the invention of printing with movable type in the fifteenth-century. Just as the latter facilitated the spread of ideas and waves of innovation in the centuries that followed, so we seem likely now to be on the threshold of another leap forward.

Triple Tsunamis provides an invaluable guide for businessmen and policymakers to the pitfalls that lie ahead and the opportunities that are beckoning in the post-crisis world."

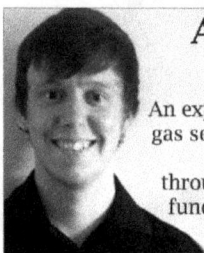

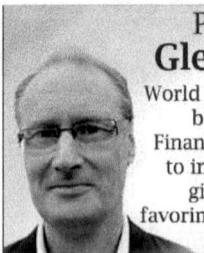

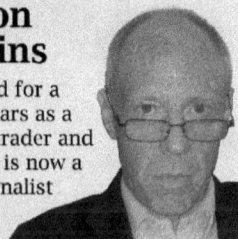

More Books from ADVFN

The Game in Wall Street

by Hoyle and Clem Chambers

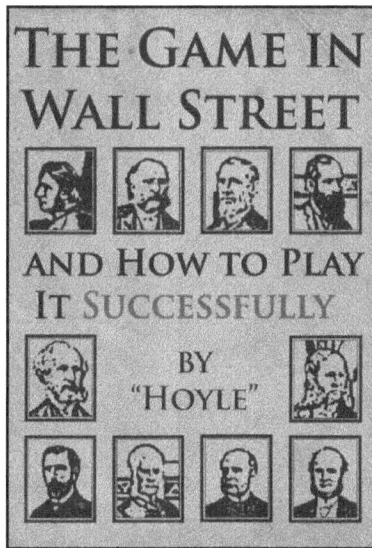

As the new century dawned, Wall Street was a game and the stock market was fixed. Ordinary investors were fleeced by big institutions that manipulated the markets to their own advantage and they had no comeback.

The Game in Wall Street shows the ways that the titans of rampant capitalism operated to make money from any source they could control. Their accumulated funds gave the titans enormous power over the market and allowed them to ensure they won the game.

Traders joining the game without knowing the rules are on a road to ruin. It's like gambling without knowing the rules and with no idea of the odds.

The Game in Wall Street sets out in detail exactly how this market manipulation works and shows how to ride the price movements and make a profit.

And guess what? The rules of the game haven't changed since the book was first published in 1898. You can apply the same strategies in your own investing and avoid losing your shirt by gambling against the professionals.

Illustrated with the very first stock charts ever published, the book contains a new preface and a conclusion by stock market guru Clem Chambers which put the text in the context of how Wall Street operates today.

The Death of Wealth

by Clem Chambers

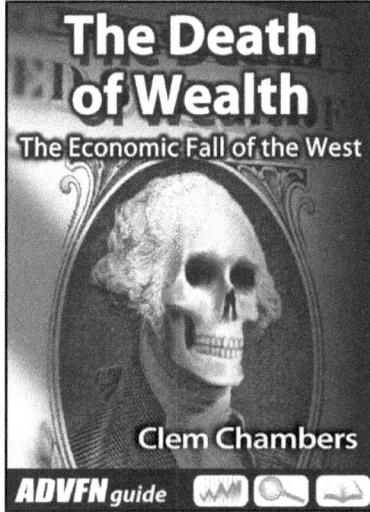

The Death of Wealth

The Economic Fall of the West

Clem Chambers

ADVFN guide

Question: what is the next economic game changer?
Answer: The Death of Wealth.

Market guru Clem Chambers dissects the global economy and the state of the financial markets and lays out the evidence for the death of wealth.

The Death of Wealth flags up the milestones on the route towards impending financial disaster. From the first tentative signs of recovery in the UK and US stock markets at the start of 2012, to the temporary drawing back from the edge of the Fiscal Cliff at the end, the book chronicles the trials and tribulations of the markets throughout the year.

Collecting together articles and essays throughout the last twelve months along with extensive new analysis for 2013, *The Death of Wealth* allows us to look at these tumultuous events collectively and draw a strong conclusion about what the future holds.

2012 started with the US economy showing signs of recovery, and European financial markets recovering some of the ground lost during the euro crisis. It ended with Obama's re-election and the deal that delayed the plunge off the fiscal cliff by a few months.

In between, the eurozone crisis continued, but none of the affected countries actually left the eurozone; quantitative easing tried to turn things around with the consequences of these "unorthodox" actions yet unknown; and the equity markets after the mid-year correction became strongly bullish.

The Death of Wealth takes you through the events of 2012 month by month, with charts showing the movements of the FTSE 100, the NASDAQ COMPX and the SSE COMPX throughout the year.

With an introduction by renowned market commentator and stock tipster Tom Winnifrith and a summary by trading technical analyst Zak Mir, this collection chronicles the rocky road trip the financial systems of the world have been on and predicts the ultimate destination: the death of wealth as we know it.

For more information go to the ADVFN Books website at www.advfnbooks.com.

ADVFN BOOKS

www.ingramcontent.com/pod-product-compliance
Lightning Source LLC
Chambersburg PA
CBHW070921270326
41927CB00011B/2667